Breaking the Silence

Tales, tips and triumphs from
an alcoholic's wife.

By

Amber Haehnel

Disclaimer:

The author has made every effort to ensure that the information in this book was correct at press time. The authors do not assume and hereby disclaim any liability to any party for any loss, damage, or disruption caused by errors or omissions, whether such errors or omissions result from accident, or any other cause.

Due to the variability of materials and skills, the author assumes no responsibility for any personal injury, property damage, or other loss of any sort suffered from any actions taken based on or inspired by information or advice herein. Make sure you completely understand any procedure before beginning work. If ever uncertain, consult a profession.

The author is not a therapist or addiction counselor, the words contained are not meant to substitute for therapy or addiction treatment.

To the lover and friend of an alcoholic (this is not just limited to married couples, or straight couples, or any other type of couple, this is for everyone with an alcoholic in their life):

You are strong and capable. You are going to make it through this. If that means sticking it out and hanging on with help, or if that means walking away, you are ok. You are going to be ok and you are strong regardless of the decisions you make.

This is not about you. No matter how hard you love someone, how much you give of yourself to them, how much you scream and nag and bitch and moan, this isn't about you. It's their disease/problem/habit. You cannot change it. I repeat this for the cheap seats in the back, you cannot change this.

You can only change yourself and you can only control yourself and your own responses. You get to choose to be happy, and you get to choose the outcome for yourself.

Always choose to love yourself first and foremost and send love out in the universe to get it in return.

This is for you. You are not alone, and you are loved.

Stigma: Noun

A mark of disgrace associated with
a particular circumstance, quality or person

Table of Contents

Introduction

On December 31st, 2018, I posted on social media a recap of my year, as most people do, to brag about all the good and get some sympathy for all the bad. Or you know, to connect with other people, or so they say.

One of the items I posted, I was incredibly proud of and grateful for and that was my husband had chosen recovery. Of course, I checked with him before posting his portion in my story, he was fine with it and off I went creating awesome words to make this accomplishment even better than it already was. I was not surprised by the outpouring of love not only based on that statement but also the other accomplishments I had throughout the year.

What I was surprised by was the six messages that came in that night and the next morning from women saying thank you for posting, from women who were silently navigating this same story, who were also the wife of an alcoholic or addict. Some of them hadn't even told their families what they were going through, shamed to the point of thinking they could not share any detail of their story with anyone...except me. What a mind-blowing moment, that people trusted me with their stories simply because I shared mine. By sharing my story and what I had been going through, they felt they could share their truth with me, to that I am incredibly grateful for the trust.

What I realized from this is the stigma surrounding addiction of any kind, the need to hide from it and hide it from anyone we know, the shame and guilt we feel just being there for someone we love, the maddening experiences we endure. If we do tell someone, the judgement that comes from telling them, the opinions of someone who has no idea what it is like, the guilt for staying. All of our experiences are so similar, most of the feeling that we are alone in this and have no one who will champion us and stand in our corner.

I am not upset about not having a champion or someone to stand in my corner, because it gave me the courage and strength to be my own champion and to stand up tall in the center of my ring, not in the corner. It also gave me the strength and courage to stand up for others, to be in their corner, to allow them to share their truth – no matter how ugly it might be, and to be the person to speak my voice so others can as well.

This one simple post on New Year's Eve completely changed my perspective on all that is living life with a loved one dealing with addiction. It completely opened my eyes to how other women silently navigate the issues of this type of relationship and feel completely alone when none of us has to be. And none of us need the guilt or shame of telling someone only to be judged or to have our spouse/friend/lover judged as well.

This post made me realize we get to break the stigma not only on addiction but on mental health, on loving someone who is addicted, on co-dependency, on relationships with addiction, on families dealing with addiction. And so many more issues that have been so taboo and stigmatized and no one seems to want to talk about it. We get to break the damn silence on all of this, we get to teach people so they understand instead of judge. We get to show what this is actually like in order to bring awareness and more intelligence to the issues.

If I were to guess, at least one person in your life is dealing with addiction, in a relationship with an addict or is struggling with mental health.

The more we talk about it, the more we can talk about it, the less people feel alone.

Let's break the silence right here and now.

Here we go.

* * *

I want to be clear on what you are about to read. This is not a "how to deal with the addict in your life" or a what to do type of thing or how to get someone to stop their addiction kind of book. I certainly hope nothing like that exists, and we can get in to that later.

This is a real life look at what this life looks like, a brutally honest version of what we go through as loved ones of addicts, specifically what a significant other goes through. This is not meant to guide you through anything, it is mean to be a sounding force for you, a support manifesto if you will, an "I got you sister, cause I am here too" kind of appreciation book.

If you are looking for a how to guide, sis, you are in the wrong mindset. That is not how this works, because there isn't one. There may be a ton of books out there talking about how to get through it, what to do, how to get them to stop, what your role is in their behavior. However, and I am saying this as loudly and boldly as possible...

This has nothing to do with you.

Yep, that's the truth. It has nothing to do with how much they love you, or how hard they want to work at the marriage or relationship, or if you are a good wife. Nope, it has nothing to do with any of those things.

You are a badass. You are still here, and therefore you are an awesome, supportive person. Stop questioning you. It's not you.

This book is my story. My story of how everything came to a head, why I chose to stay, why I still choose to stay and how I realized this is not about me – at all. This is my story of what I learned, and am still learning. And this is the story I put out in to the world so other women know they are not alone, and my wish is that a light can be shone down on the subject of addiction so it is not such a taboo and stigmatized subject anymore.

I want to make this clear before you continue, I believe alcoholism is a disease, a family disease, meaning the entire family is involved and needs to seek help in the process. I believe it is inherent and can be treated, thought it cannot be cured.

I also made the choice, and still make the choice every day, to stay in my marriage. I made the choice to get through it and make it work regardless of what that means. And I encourage women to do the same, as long as the situation is safe, to at least try.

However, whether you choose to stay or leave, I will never judge you, and I believe you should continue getting help, the effects of this last a lifetime and it is important, whether you are still with the person or not, to make sure you are taking care of yourself first and foremost.

One last thing - I am not a therapist or a counselor. This book is strictly my experiences, my opinions and what I have learned in an effort to help someone else along the way. I will always encourage to the fullest of my abilities for every person to go to a therapist and work through their own issues.

Chapter 1

We all have a history...

We all have one, and this book could only start with mine. I have a history with alcohol as I am sure most of us do.

The first time I got drunk was when I was sixteen, at a hotel party, on apple pucker. Apple Pucker you guys. I was totally classy. Who the hell even drinks this stuff straight?? A sixteen-year-old.

After this, I drank sometimes because it was super cool, right? Parties, friends' houses, whatever the case might be, I wanted to be the cool kid. I even kept little air plane bottles of vodka in my closet in case I needed to look even cooler. Cause that's totally the case. No one ever even knew they were there, unless of course my mom found them at some point, because I have no idea where they went. Maybe my brother found them at some point and thought I was super cool but never admitted it.

After high school I moved to Las Vegas. I had no friends, no social life and fully focused on work and school. Until I met the friends.

I met a friend – who I will talk more about later – and we met for drinks. Met for drinks, I felt so damn sophisticated. I was scared to even drink, I hadn't ever socially drank before, but there we were. I joined a bowling league with some super cool dudes and that quickly became a drinking league that happened to bowl on Saturday nights.

Enter the kickball league. Damn, so much drinking. I think to the point we all quit a couple of years later because it was so much drinking. And parties, and after parties, and all the things. I felt like the greatest social butterfly ever. And, really at the time, we all were. It was wonderful.

And here's the thing, I didn't even like alcohol. I really didn't even like drinking all that much, there a few specific liquors at this point I cannot even smell without wanting to vomit. I lost control – which to a control freak is not the greatest thing in the world – and the next day started feeling worse and worse, the joys of growing older in this area. My skin was shit, I ate like shit and therefore felt like shit. But I just kept going. As we all do, especially in those early 20's, we want to be all about everything and fit in with everyone.

Honestly, drinking is how I met my husband, and how we bonded at first. A friend invited me over for drinks, there's that social que again, and introduced me to him. After that we would meet for dinners now and then which always included alcohol, and he drank quite a bit so I felt like I needed to as well, you know, to fit in.

All of this was all fun...until it wasn't. That's how it rolls, things are super fun until they aren't anymore and you realize the impact they are actually having on your life.

It wasn't until my birthday in 2018, after my husband had chosen recovery, after he had relapsed, after all the drama of getting to the point he knew it was an issue, that I decided I was done. A super easy feat for me, I wish it were as easy for everyone. I just decided I was done after a headache the day after my birthday, and that was that. I will say this here, if you can choose to stop drinking, if you can pick up one drink and not continue after that, if you can choose to never drink again in your life....that is a fucking privilege and I hope you understand that. If not, we will get in to it later.

There were several reasons I chose to stop drinking. Yes, one of those reasons was in support of my husband and his recovery. But there are so many more, I was sick of feeling like shit, I was definitely done with migraines (which are the devil working I swear), I was tired of crappy skin, of all the side effects that alcohol provide for me. Maybe some of you don't experience this, but I sure as shit do and I was tired of it. Not to mention, I started to hate, loathe with my whole being, alcohol.

I know that's not necessarily fair, but alcohol had only caused bull shit in my life, it never did anything good for me, I started to hate it with every ounce of who I am. I kept that thought to myself for fear of sounding like an absolute insane person – which maybe I am, but I am a sober one anyway.

This is a super brief history of my relationship with alcohol. We definitely had our ups and downs and broke up a couple of times after some super bad hangovers. Those of you in your early 20's bragging about how you don't have hangovers, neither did I. Your late 20's will hit you like a freaking freight train. You have been warned, you are not immune.

8

I don't want to hate alcohol, it helped me bond with new friends, helped me out when I was nervous to do something, was along for the ride as my husband and I started actually dating. And sweet Moscato I really freaking loved you.

However, the bad with alcohol definitely outweighed the good in my case. This was the best option for me, not for anyone else. I don't expect anyone to stop drinking if it is controlled and what they want to do. I don't expect anyone to take this as I will not be around alcohol, if that's your thing and you are good with it, by all means, let's go out, hang out, hell even come over to my house for some dinner and bring it along. Just take it with you when you leave.

Here's what's up, don't judge my decisions and I will not judge yours. Cool?

Sweet. Let's get this party started.

Chapter 2

And we function.

Ever heard the term "functioning alcoholic"? I have, so many times I could burn my ears if I heard it again. This is what my husband was classified as.

He had a great job, he maintained social relationships, he was happy for the most part and enjoyed life. He was far from the stereotype surrounding alcoholics, and it is my belief that most are. For the most part, no one on the outside really recognizes or notices there is a problem.

For a long time, I found myself lucky. I heard horror stories of alcoholic relationships and how bad they really get. There is physical abuse and child abuse and all sorts of horrible incidents, getting courts and jails and stalking involved.

Not the case here. As much as he may have been classified a functioning alcoholic, we also had a functioning relationship. We were happy on the outside and only a tiny, close fraction of the people we knew understood what was happening in our relationship. On the outside, we looked pretty happy, but inside our closed doors, we were just functioning.

I was pushing so hard for him to stop drinking and get help, and he was therefore pushing so hard against it. It felt like there was constantly this elephant in the room, and it was mostly sitting on top both of us. That's what this felt like, hardly able to breathe and always on edge.

I would come home, no matter the day I had, always happy to be home, however the second I walked in and realized he was drunk, my mood immediately dissolved to despair and anger. I was angry so much of the time, and I started to retreat because of it. I had the urge to run away the second I saw him, and though these words may be hard for him to read, it was the truth. I wanted to retreat to a safe place where I did not have to worry whether I was going to deal with the drunk guy tonight.

I was guilty, because who was I to complain when other people had it so much worse in an alcoholic relationship. I had it pretty good. Drunk husband was hilarious, he was always cracking jokes, he clung on to me and made me the most important person ever. How could I really be complaining??

Well, because drunk guy also had super inappropriate humor that was super embarrassing most of time. He clung to me, but it wasn't out of love and made me feel like the only way he could be around me was if he had knocked a few back first. Drunk version would talk – like a lot – and say the same things over and over again and then get mad if I stopped listening. He was super irritable and got offended quickly. Again, this is not an attack on him, it was just the version of him I grew to dislike so much the word divorce flew out of my mouth quicker than any other word. Tears filled my eyes so often; I really did not know what it felt like to not cry for an entire day. Most of the time, I would cry in the shower, or in the car on my way home from work so he didn't see it. I hated crying in front of him, because when I did, his feelings seemed to go from cold, to colder.

I know now when I expressed my emotion, it was reflecting on him and he dismissed it. I also have learned since then, he is just really not an expressive person, at the time I blamed everything, including his innate behavior on alcohol. I had no clue who he truly was when he was sober. I had no idea who he could be. I just knew this version of him. The guy I was growing more quickly away from and I feeling less and less sad about the entire relationship imploding.

That's when it gets really tough. When you honestly feel in your heart you don't have anything more left to give. There is nothing left in there, you have fought the good fight and now you can barely hold yourself up, let alone an entire relationship all by yourself. At this point, I knew it was over. I knew I couldn't go on any further.

That's when he decided to change. More on that later.

For those of you with a functioning relationship, this is what I have to offer:

Again, counseling/therapy. That will honestly be my go-to always. It changed the entire course of my life and I am a diehard advocate.

A relationship is only as good as the two parts in it, and you cannot do it alone. It is just not possible. You can for a while but eventually you will start to be worn down by the weight of it all. If this happens, take a break. Don't make a hasty decision, take a break for yourself, breathe and figure out what you want and how much you can handle. If you are at your breaking point and can do no more...look in to separation.

Stop trying to impress or put on a show for other people. I am not suggesting you take your problems public; however, I am suggesting you do things that will make you happy by yourself. You don't always have to put on a show and you deserve happiness and something for you.

Your situation is yours. If you are unhappy it doesn't matter what other people are going through, and comparing yourself is the ultimate form of torture. Just be in your relationship. Do not ever feel guilty because someone might have it worse. There are always going to be people that have it better than we do and unfortunately there will always be people who have it worse. Put your blinders on and stay in your own lane.

Chapter 3

Better or Worse

I think I am really funny. Like the kind of funny that gets to other people and makes them lighter in their heart, or pisses them off. One or the other.

No, this is not a chapter on marriage and loving someone through all of the good and bad. This is not about accepting someone for better or worse until you die.

This chapter is about the fact – yes, it is a fact – that nothing you do will make this situation better or worse. Nothing you do is going to change what another person does in general, but especially here. You cannot change another person's behavior no matter how hard you try, and the more you try, the more you will make yourself crazy. The more you will ruin your own relationship with yourself.

So, yes, there are things you can do to make your relationship better, and things you can do to make it worse. From your end of things. I am going to say this again for the cheap seats in the back – You cannot control someone else's behavior. We struggle enough in life, there is no need to make it worse by trying to control another person.

You can take steps to make things better – you can go to therapy, work on being compassionate for yourself, work on detachment and get help – all of these things will make it better. They will make life in general better, and that is just good all around.

You can make things worse – by being miserable, by sulking, by yelling and causing a scene, by destroying your own self-love by enveloping yourself in to someone else's life and behaviors.

But nothing, I will repeat, nothing you do will make someone drink more or less. Nothing you do or do not do will make someone behave in a certain way. Nothing you do or don't do will change someone. Except yourself. You can change yourself at any point in time. You can determine whether you will indulge in activities that are unhealthy for you. You can determine whether you will behave in a certain way. You can decide if you will or will not change.

Get it? It is up to you to change you. It is up to you to take care of yourself and be in control of yourself and only you. That is the only thing you can control – your responses and your attitude, so do well to maintain both and keep control of yourself.

Anything outside of that will not be productive for you or anyone else. And I promise you, it will only hinder your relationship, especially with an addict.

Better or worse, it is up to you.

No matter how hard you try, you cannot control when your loved one drinks. I tried controlling this for years, if I followed him everywhere, watched his every move – hell, if I checked his phone, as if that had anything to do with it. I even thought about telling him I would take him to and from work. What?! He would never agree to that, luckily, and can you imagine? He would feel like a prisoner and I would be so ridden with stress and anxiety always, no to mention never living my own damn life.

Which is what I did – for a long time. I lived solely to find out if he drank, my days were wrapped up in whether or not he had a drink, how many, and what he was going to do about it. I lived his life, only the way I thought it should be lived. I grilled him with questions constantly. I wrapped all of my emotions around how he was that day.

I would literally wait until I found out if he drank that day to figure out if I was happy or sad. And if he hadn't, I still wasn't happy just kind of floating through, like a somewhat mused solemn person. If he had, well there were all the emotions; sad, angry, frustrated, exhausted, furious, upset for him, disappointed, you name it. And it would all hit me at once and then it would all hit him at once. I would yell and curse and call names and scream and be pissed and then cry like I had never cried before.

There was a night I threw up – just from crying so horrifically.

I would try everything I could to control him. This did not work. Right now, I want you to know, this does not work – it makes things so much worse, not only for them but for you as well. If you are trying to control the situation just know, you will never be able to and in the meantime you will more than likely ruin not only whatever is left of your sanity, but also whatever is left of the relationship. And there is hope here. When you give up control, so many things start to change.

You no longer feel that stress and anxiety over the day – don't get me wrong here, this doesn't disappear immediately, it takes time but it does start to fall away. You no longer worry about what someone else is doing – this also takes some practice – and you get to start focusing on things you enjoy, the things you want to do, which in turn makes you such a happier person. You eventually start to feel more gratitude and happiness.

You are able to deal with what comes your way in much calmer manner. Again, it doesn't happen overnight. I have been practicing this for a long while now and just two weeks ago had a blow up fit for war on my husband. It takes time and then you screw up and it takes some time again.

Here's the thing, I never feel good after I blow up. I never feel good after screaming and yelling, if you do, I don't know, you might need a little extra therapy. Yelling sometimes let us release some tension, but for the most part, it just makes us feel like shit afterward. You know when I feel good? After I have kept my cool. After I have walked away from a shitty situation, after I have taken time to breathe. That is when I feel really good, and I want more of that in my life these days, so that is what I will focus more on.

Of course, we all fuck up from time to time. We work really hard to reach a certain point and then oops, we completely revert back because our brains go there. It's ok. Just keep moving, keep going, keep telling yourself who you are and who you want to be. It takes a whole lotta freaking time. And a whole lotta freaking work.

Aren't you ready to finally feel good instead of stressed, anxious and overwhelmed? Start working on being good to you, doing what you want in life and less focus on anyone else. And practice, you will get there. You will probably take a few steps back again, and have to start building up, but that is what this is about, being able to see when you take a step back and build back up from there.

You cannot control this, and you cannot make them better or worse. However, you have the choice to make this either better or worse for yourself. Which do you choose?

Chapter 4

A Million Reasons

I had a dream last night that I was on the Ellen show. The freaking Ellen show you guys! But wait, there's more. Not only was I dreaming I was on the Ellen show talking about my experiences and my book, but I was also describing how much I love the one and only Stefani Germanotta – THE Lady Gaga herself and how much she has helped me in this journey. Just then, she announced she had a surprise for me. If you know the Ellen Show, you know what the surprise was. Lady Gaga herself.

We sat next to one another, holding hands and crying over all the things we have been through and how similar we are. Then I woke up. I woke up feeling amazing by the way. It's not every day you meet both Ellen and Lady Gaga, even it is just in a dream.

It was either my total obsession with the Mother Monster or the fact that I knew she needed mention in this book that has consumed my mind, whichever, that dream was freaking awesome!

During any hard time, or any good time it was her music that soothed me and seemed to speak right to my soul. I would quote lyrics and put them up as reminders on how to go about my day. Music and I have a very special relationship. For the most part, my mood can be easily detected by the type of music I am currently listening to. And I listen for the message, the meaning and the melody that really speaks to me.

But one spoke to me the most. The song Million Reasons. Damn. I even played it for my husband at one point, to which he asked if he was that bad. Yep. And that good. Ill explain.

The million reasons – the lies, the manipulation, the hiding, the lies, the manipulation, the let downs, the lies. The many, many lies.

But one good reason – one good time, one smile, one good day, one sober day, one show of promise, one show of a good future – just one. That one good reason is what we stay for, what we strive for and what we want more than anything. It gives us hope and promise to hold on to. And sometimes that hope and promise is all we need to endure the reasons that make us want to let go. Sometimes that hope and promise is the part that makes us stay when we shouldn't. Sometimes it's just not enough, and sometimes it is. And sometimes you just don't fucking know which way is up or down, and drift a little.

Ever have those thoughts of "if I just didn't have to deal with this anymore, everything would be perfectly ok"? I did, a lot. That's when I would blast songs like this and probably cry in my car. Now I am going to say the hard part. This isn't the only bad thing in your life. Sure, it can feel like it is ever consuming and the worst thing in your life and if you just walked away from it, everything would somehow magically align and things would be all sunshine and rainbows. However, it is not your only issue. It is not the only thing going south in your life.

It is really easy to blame everything in your life, especially the bad, on this one issue, not to mention the person doing it. It is so easy to blame them for everything. I blamed my husband for terrible traffic and getting home late, for any bad mood I had, for a bad day at work, the list could go on and on and on, and none of it was his fault. Even in the good times, it is so tough to let that wall down and just be happy, and so easy to blame them for that. Sometimes it would feel like the hardest thing and exhausting work just to appear happy.

And all it took was one reason, to make it all better.

I put my happiness in someone else's hands, in someone's hands who couldn't figure out happiness for themselves, yet I gave him the task of figuring it out for me as well. How fair is that? It's not. Not even a little.

I kept thinking if he would give me that one little reason, continuing sobriety, it would be the one thing that would magically change all my bad days, the traffic, my job, all of it. With a decision he would make, it would change my whole life. What pressure that is, I can feel it now just writing this. The pressure of holding someone else's good days and happiness in your hands when you are also attempting to figure out your own shit? Wow. And I did that. Both to him and myself. I was destroying two people.

But how can it work both directions? In many ways, his addiction was the downfall of my own life, it destroyed me – each time he relapsed – it destroyed me, it made me lose trust, it made me lose a little love, it made me feel second best and worthless. So, if it can make me feel all the bad, how can him stopping not make me feel all the good?

That question I will answer later, because it is a long answer. But the main point here is that my happiness and my own recovery as a spouse is my responsibility and mine only. What he does in his life, and the decisions he makes about his own life are not mine, I cannot control them and in the same line, they cannot control me. That is so tough to swallow, but it is the truth and what made everything change for me.

Taking control of my happiness and my decisions about how I would respond to any and everything – including drinking – were mine. It was so freeing to finally realize that. And it took a while, I am still practicing this actually, because it is so tough. I definitely still had moments of screaming, I still had bad days that I blamed on him, I still was angry and resentful, but I was working so hard on myself that all of these things drifted away slowly. I felt myself not yelling quite as much and instead taking a moment so I could respond. I found myself taking time for myself in general, just so I could reflect on myself and how I wanted to be. I found myself having more good days, because regardless of what he was doing, I was making it a good day. I found myself not trying to figure out his every move, not trying to smell is breath when I got home, not watching his behaviors searching for something that was off. It took some real time, and still does, but I am getting there. And it makes it so much easier to just be myself and be happy.

I still get sad and frustrated and angry, and all of those things are natural human emotions and we are allowed to experience them all. However, I check my reactions and attempt to respond. And I know I am in control of the emotions I am feeling, no one else. And I work on checking myself when I am feeling a sort of way.

If I am feeling sad or angry, I allow myself to feel that way — alone. I allow myself to feel the emotions I need to feel so that I do not take happiness for granted. If I get frustrated, I get down to why I am really feeling that way and if it won't matter later that day, I do my best to let it go.

And I listen to music, almost always, any time I can, I listen to something that inspires me, or something that seems to just get me in some way, something that allows my anger to come out. Oh, and I work out, cause you know, endorphins and all that.

All you need is one good reason to stick around, to keep someone in your life. The point here is, you cannot force someone to give you that reason, they get to make up their minds all on their own. And the more you attempt to force them, the further they typically move away. It is on you to make yourself happy, and it is really unfair to put that responsibility in someone else's hands, especially when that someone may not even know how to make themselves happy.

Wake up to what is going on and to how you feel about it. If you do not like something, stop putting up with it. This does not mean to leave the person — unless abuse is happening, in that case please do and please get help immediately — it means to start taking accountability for yourself and be responsible for you and you only. You cannot change someone, no matter how hard you try, and again the more you try the less likely you are to make it happen. However, you can change yourself, at any point you decide to. And that is the point here, you making yourself happy. You giving yourself that one reason to stay, you letting go of the million reasons. And most importantly, you not becoming a doormat for anyone.

Chapter 5

Shame is a four-letter word.

Let's talk about the perception of what an alcoholic looks like. Maybe angry, dirty, homeless, frustrated, hates the world, a bad person? Someone who cannot control themselves?

Some, sure. But that is true with any person in our population regardless of addiction. Now, let's talk about what an alcoholic really looks like – the reality. Every person. Every personality. Every type of job, every walk of life, every single person. There is no certain way an alcoholic or addict looks or acts.

My husband was happy, he very rarely got angry at much of anything – he did and does get frustrated, but really, who the hell doesn't get frustration from time to time in life? He was happier when he was drinking for sure, he made jokes, he was the life of the party. He didn't yell or cause a scene – well, until it got a little worse and he stopped caring if he caused a scene. He held down a badass job and kept up with social engagements, family events, my events, all of them. He did not meet the stereotypical standards of what an alcoholic is.

And for a long time, we hid.

I hid that he had a problem, even though most people already knew he did. I hid that I had feelings about it, I protected him and us to the best of my abilities in all thing's life. I wanted no one to know anything that was going on.

We had a fight, the first time I found out he was hiding alcohol in the house, two weeks before our wedding. It was by far the worst fight we had since we had started dating. I was crying so hard I couldn't breathe and he was going on about how he was doing nothing wrong, I couldn't understand. And you think for a second I was going to allow anyone in the world to know about this? Two weeks before our wedding? Hell no. To the outside world we were perfect and excited and getting ready to welcome our family in town and get hitched. Privately I begged him for months not to be drunk during our ceremony. I had been begging him for months – alone – to please stop drinking so much. I had no clue how bad it really was at the time.

Why didn't I reach out? Why did I not tell someone I trusted, or at the very least talk to someone to just vent out the frustrations? I will tell you exactly why. Fucking shame. That little word that comes with a gigantic feeling and even bigger weight on your shoulders.

I honestly thought I was protecting both of us, keeping it such a secret and never letting anyone in. I didn't want people to think badly of him, because he is by far the best human I know, and mostly, selfishly I didn't want people to think badly of me for staying in a relationship, or for going deeper in to commitment in that relationship by getting married. I didn't want the judgement of him, myself or our relationship. So duh, keep quiet.

Except I started feeling more and more shame and embarrassment and guilt. I started become extremely resentful and angry. I started talking about it only to bitch about it which gave the perception that I was super unhappy and that he was a monster – neither of which were true. I only told my side of the story and honestly probably picked the wrong people to tell because they encouraged me to give up and leave. Neither of which I wanted to do. Telling someone is important, but telling the right people is even more important. And I was ashamed so I wanted the toxic negativity to help me with that. Isn't it strange how we sometimes crave what is terrible for us?

So, I was becoming more and more angry and resentful, and that shame just would not go away. So instead of getting help, I started becoming a person I never knew I could be. I let go of shame for anger. I let go of embarrassment for resentment. I started calling him out in public. I started saying things to him when he was around other people about his drinking. I stopped assisting in any way, and I started using my yelling voice much more often. I started picking fights about anything and everything just so I could let out some anger.

Then came the day I left. St. Patricks' day. I will never forget it. I took off, and I ended up at my office because I really didn't know where else to go. I had food poisoning so I really needed to be near a bathroom, and I just went and work and scrolled Facebook and enjoyed the quiet office that was a second home. I honestly would have spent the night there had it been hospitable to sleep. There was a shower there though, so I considered it. I ended up at my dads' after my husband had gone over looking for me and had a talk with my dad about his plan to get sober. I was so angry I didn't even want to talk to my parents. I felt like they had betrayed me by even talking to him.

They had called me about ten times before I answered and let them know I was ok. They asked me to at least come stay with them. I was so angry and fed up I didn't even want to hear about his plans to get sober, I didn't want to hear anything, I just wanted to be silent, sleep and mindlessly watch television. So, I did.

I went home the next day to tell him he needed to leave, which he did. That Monday he showed up in the morning – once again, I had taken the morning off for myself and he disrupted it. For what seemed like the longest time, any time I took off work was to take care of him. I was furious. He cried and told me he was getting help and he had to go today. Of course, I was hesitant but so happy he decided on it.

Guess who I told? My dad. He obviously knew the plan before I did and that was that. Guess who I wanted to tell? Everyone. I wanted to shout it from the rooftops, but that mother fucking shame. It was so present. As we sat in the emergency room waiting for someone to come talk to him, it was even more present. When the nurses were so kind, and accommodating, and asked me if I wanted a blanket. Fuck. The same. I felt like I was being so judged and I just wanted to escape. I just wanted to run away, but I didn't. He wasn't running away and this was so much scarier to him, there was no way I could.

And after he got well? I still wasn't much talking about it. I still don't think he has told many people he went to detox – and reminder to make sure he is cool with me writing about it here. And it all comes back to shame.

I shamed him constantly in this journey. I would judge, and I know he could feel it. When he would make decisions, I know he could feel the weight of my judgment on him. That is why he started hiding it, that is why he stopped being honest about, he could feel me shaming him for it, making it worse.

Now, this is not to say that you have the power to make someone else's addiction worse, that is so untrue, but my shaming and judgement did very little to help the situation at all. It made our home and my love for him a completely unsafe place when it should be the safest place for him to be. It made our relationship an unsafe place altogether for him. He makes the choice to tell the truth or not, he makes the choices to drink or not, but how comfortable would you feel if someone made you feel so ashamed for what you were doing? I am going to guess not so great.

I had to look inside and learn how to be the wife of an alcoholic, because it is so different than being the wife of a non-alcoholic/addict. I had to learn how to speak to him, how to control my actions and responses, and how to love him the way he needed to be loved. Honestly, if every person went through this type of learning process, I feel like the divorce rate would go down tremendously. Any type of therapy and twelve step programs would be helpful for any single person on the planet. I can get in to that a little more later.

I had to learn what shame actually means and what I can do to help my husband and progress our marriage. I had to learn what it means to be an alcoholic and my role as a spouse to be my own person while also being supportive. I had to learn how to detach, which feels really odd at first, because being married for me initially meant being attached. I had to learn that detachment means allowing the person you love to live their own life and pave their own way, and not trying to control that. See the chapter on control, it just never works.

All of this to say, our society is what makes this feel shameful. Our society and lack of education is what makes people have a certain perception of what an alcoholic/addict looks like. Our society and lack of education is what makes me feel ashamed as a wife. This is painted in such a light that it is not right and a terrible situation. But there is no shame in this. Ill say it again, there is no shame in this. No one has to feel shame about something they cannot control on their own. And I truly believe an alcoholic cannot control this on their own. Addiction creeps in when we are alone, when it stays silent, when we hide it, because it can feed on those feelings, it can grow when we are silent. Addiction wants us to stay silent. And shame helps in that.

But there is no shame in this. No shame in staying married when you know you have a wonderful person. No shame in getting divorced when you have done all you can do. No shame in letting go and detaching. No shame in addiction at all. Shame is a four-letter word and I am determined to stop the shame, bring it to light to combat the darkness and let people know they are not alone.

Shame is a dirty fucking four letter word and it is up to all of us to stop the shame in the world and start helping people. To reach out when we can, educate ourselves so we are not ignorant to what this is, and practice some damn compassion already. Everyone is going through something, and no one needs to deal with shame on top of that.

Chapter 6

Not My Problem

Well, I don't have to stop drinking, it's not my problem. Oh, lawd. First of all, if you are thinking this, you are definitely not alone. This was my first thought when my husband checked in to detox. Actually, the night he went in I sat on the couch by myself and had a glass of wine. I enjoyed every moment, every sip, I was so happy to not be weighed down with wondering what I was coming home to, or what type of mood I needed to be in. And to know he was in good hands, I just felt free and light. Lighter than I had in a long time. I savored every second. That may make me a horrible person, but I really don't care if it does. I will happily admit my feelings that night.

I even had friends asking me, well you are not going to stop drinking, are you? As if that was some sort of social suicide – don't stop drinking, lord no! It's not your problem. And I felt the same way. I didn't get myself in to this, I didn't have a problem with alcohol, I don't need to stop doing it. Fuck you, husband. I almost wanted to make a point that I could still drink, and show off that I didn't have an addiction to alcohol, what an ass hole I was. I almost wanted to rub it in, he caused me pain with this whole thing, so I was going to do it right back to him. Yea, I was definitely an ass hole. And listening way too much to people who had zero idea of what I was going through.

Here's a clue. Unless someone has been through what you are going through, you might want to not fully listen to their advice on the situation. One of my favorite quotes is Dave Ramsey, don't take advice from broke people. That's how I feel in this. Don't take advice from people who have no idea. I have an idea, so take my advice here. Another favorite of mine is a mix from Teddy Roosevelt and Brene Brown, and it is something like this: if you are not in the arena getting your ass kicked, I am not open to or interested in your feedback on my work. Bam.

I started to feel massive guilt. Not often, but maybe a handful of times I met up with some friends and he opted to stay home. I started feeling tremendous guilt if I went out without him and chose to have a drink. And I would try my hardest not to talk about it when I got home. I would sneak in to bed and feel so guilty. He had the option to come with me, and decided not to, but damn, the guilt. Nothing good can bring this much guilt.

Even at home, he would make it very clear he did not mind if I had a glass of wine. He kept telling me he did not care if I had a drink. But, deep down I knew he did.

He told me when we were engaged, he didn't care if I took his last name or not. I knew it wasn't true. He is the kind of person that just wants to keep the peace. He just wants everyone around him to be content and doesn't like commotion. He would rather be disappointed and upset than to put that on someone else. It's just who he is. This is also why he would lie about drinking; he did not want me to be disappointed or upset and thought he could hide it. This was a long drawn out conversation we had, and it seemed like a complete contradiction but it made perfect sense. I digress.

I had the attitude that it was not my issue, so I did not need to stop. And I am going to say now, I was wrong. I was completely wrong. This is my issue. I truly believe addiction is a family disease and it effects every single person in the family. It is my issue; it is something I got to reevaluate in my own life.

After I got out of my own damn way, and put my ego aside and realized that I don't, in fact, want to hurt him at all, I don't want to put it in his face, I don't want to make this harder. I thought I did, but that is shit, I didn't want to. I hurt so I wanted him to hurt as well. Hurt people hurt people.

After I got all of that out, I started thinking about what I actually want in my life. What do I want to do, regardless of anything we are going through in our marriage, regardless of what issues I have or he has? What do I really want in life? What do I really want my life to look like? Does alcohol actually play a part in that?

And the answer to that last question was no. Here's the thing, I always had regrets after I drank, I always felt like shit, physically yes, but more so I felt like shit about myself internally. And it gave me a massive migraine, sometimes for days. Not something I need in my life. If you get migraines, you know, we do everything we can to prevent yourself from getting these little ass holes from coming on, so eliminating alcohol should have been my first thought here. I did not like the way alcohol made me feel at all, except when I was in the middle of the fun. If I was being honest with myself, I didn't like the way alcohol tasted at all. It gave me chills and I rarely actually enjoyed it. It was the social norm, and so it's what I did.

Some girlfriends surprised me for my birthday, and we went to dinner. I ordered a beer taster there, and I was not a fan of most of them, so I tried them all and proceeded to order a hard cider. I drank it, sat there and realized; this is it. I am done. And I was. I know this drives my husband crazy, and I am sure it drives anyone with an addiction to alcohol crazy. But that night I decided I was done, and I stopped. It has been almost a year since that night. Not a drink since, and no, it still hasn't been easy, even for a normie like me.

I still had moments when I thought to myself, damn it would be nice to have a drink, or to go and enjoy a cocktail, but then I would remind myself how I really don't like it anyway. I do like the social aspect of drinking, but I loathe the fact that it is so accepted that it seems odd someone isn't drinking alcohol.

Here is my biggest tip about alcohol in general: if someone says no thanks to your offering of alcohol, or avoids a night out at an alcohol related or heavy event, don't ask why. Do not question their response or decision, simply offer them something else. That's it. It's that simple.

Second tip: Stop asking women who do not drink if they are pregnant. These two are completely separate topics. Thanks in advance.

Now, my relationship with alcohol has never been a great one, and you would think eliminating it from my life would mean that relationship somehow became better but this is far from the case. I have gone through moments where I hate alcohol, I hate that it exists, I hate that it is so accepted and accessible, I hate that I have lost so many people in my life to fucking alcohol. To this substance that everyone just does without a care in the world, that people put so much pressure on others to do, that people talk about as if it is some sort of a badge of honor. It took the lives of people I love, was on its way to taking my husbands' and damn near destroyed our marriage.

I hate it. With a fiery passion. Most of the time.

That being said I want to make something else very clear. This is MY relationship with alcohol, this is what has happened in my life, and my experience. This is all mine, and it has nothing to do with you.

I am not judging you for your alcohol consumption, nor do I not want to be invited to your birthday party because I don't drink. Nope, I still want to be included. I still want to enjoy the good times with you and sit with you in the bad, and for me, that doesn't involve alcohol, but if it does for you, awesome. I am not here to judge you or preach to you. I am simply here to tell my story and what I have been through in the hopes it will help someone else. I am not some prude that can't stand the look of you drinking. Do you. Live your damn life. I want to still be a part of it.

It was almost as if we became social pariahs, all of a sudden people no longer wanted to come over or if they did they actually asked their significant other when they could leave to go have "real fun", yea we heard you, you know who you are.

And I still love you. No one invited us over anymore, or invited us out. And if we were invited out, or invited others out, there were all sorts of questions – well we are going to drink, is that cool? - of course, it's fucking cool, we are not in charge of your life. Or finding things to do outside of drinking or going to a bar – not easy when you live in Las Vegas, but also, it's kind of easy it's just no one wanted to. At the end of the day, we realized we had some super awesome friends and some people we really needed to let go of, and that is totally okay. We are not here to please others, we are here to live the best lives for ourselves, and if that means we have to leave some people on their own path, that is completely cool. It just really sucked that alcohol was the reason.

I also got so much shit right after Chad got back from detox, with the very few people who knew about it. "it's not your problem, come out anyway", "he has to figure this out at some point," "what are you going to do, be hermits for the rest of your lives?" Damn people. Let others make their own decisions for themselves, because honestly, all of those were shitty questions which led to shitty responses and shitty decisions. My decisions are my own and I will never blame anyone else for them, but sometimes you might just need someone who supports and at the very least tries to understand. Try to be that person for someone else.

And if me not drinking makes you uncomfortable, well, friend, that is your fucking problem, not mine. And maybe our friendship should be reevaluated.

At the end of the day, it is my problem because I choose to be this man's wife. I choose to be by his side. It is my problem, and damn, being sober actually feels pretty fucking great.

Chapter 7

No more hiding out.

I can't tell you the amount of time I spent in hiding. The amount of time I spent covering up our problems and not allowing anyone in to help, or to understand, or worse – to judge. I spent so much time not having anyone in my corner and not talking to anyone, when I could have.

I blame myself but I also blame shame. It is difficult to tell your story when it involves someone else's story so intensely. You somewhat need to ask for permission to share your own feelings, or to talk to others because in doing that, you expose them to so much. Not on purpose, but my story is intertwined with my husbands, it is difficult without his support. Luckily, I get to share what I need to with his full support.

This is for me to heal, and hopefully help someone else know they are not alone. This is such a lonely thing to go through. As a spouse or family member we feel like we cannot express our own feelings, thoughts, opinions, because we are all about them getting better. It seems selfish to say you have feelings about this or talk about how it has impacted your own life. It isn't about us; it is all about them. This is so far from the truth. There is so much that impacts our lives, our thoughts, our minds, everything. And we rarely get to share all of that.

For the most part, in the beginning, I was not sharing much of our lives out of shame and embarrassment. Both for myself and for him. I did not want people to judge this person, I wanted to protect him and keep him safe from the judgement of others. I wanted to keep myself safe from the judgement of others. I hid so well I even lost a lot of who I am in the process. I got so good at putting on that fake smile, and avoiding the issue it made me in to a completely different person. And I was miserable on the inside. I was so tired of being alone in this, I was so sick of pretending to be happy and putting on a show, I just stopped wanting to be around people at all. I was sick of hiding my feelings about alcohol, mostly when I was around it, it would actually make me physically sick.

I felt like if I complained about our marriage and about alcohol people would judge me for sticking around. If it was so bad, just get out. So, I hid. I made myself sick both mentally and physically, I lost so much self-esteem, and was in such a bad place. All because I was so terrified of people knowing my truth.

As time went on, I started sharing a little more and a little more – only with people I felt like I could trust exclusively. I was met with the questions of why I stayed and people telling me I should get out now while it was still new. Here's the thing, I didn't want to get out of my marriage. I loved this man and I knew his potential, and that is the only thing that had me holding on. He was and is the best human I know, and I know his true heart, and that is what kept me where I was. I didn't want to give up on him or us. So of course, these comments just hit me hard. They did get me thinking several times why I was staying. In the end I knew I was getting advice from the wrong people, especially when I didn't ask for it. Which made that dark place I was in even darker.

I started attending some Al-anon meetings and at first, I was simply in the wrong group. I felt like it was just a bashing session and it was so unproductive for my brain at the time. Luckily, I found a new group that is amazing and I was able to share without fear of judgment and with people who understood was I was going through and were not first to ask why I was staying. This did a huge amount of good for my mental well-being, and I highly recommend anyone in this situation to find a group for support. A group of people who actually understand appreciate what you are going through, it changed so much in my life.

Eventually, I learned to be more authentic to myself and stop caring what other people thought of me, my husband or my marriage. The tricky thing with addiction, whether you are the addict or a loved one, is it loves to be alone. Addiction thrives in the dark and it most certainly thrives when you feel like there is no one else there for you. It wants you to feel separate. It wants you to feel desperate. It is when you bring in the light and realize you are most certainly not alone in this is when you really start to wake up.

You start to see that embarrassment is not something to be feared. At least I did.

I posted on social media on New Year's Eve that my husband had chosen recovery that year. It was the first time I really let my walls down and was honest with a large audience. The response was exactly why I posted. Six different women messaged me that night, sharing their truth with me that they were going through the exact same situation in silence. They didn't want anyone to know about it and they were at their wits end. Some of them were dealing with loneliness so fierce it made them want to take their own lives. That is some real shit, and it really happens. You start to feel so let down and useless you get in to a super dark place and have no idea how to get out of it. It took my breath away that me sharing this fact, and allowing those walls to come down and be authentic in sharing myself that other people were able to reach out to me as their first step in finding help. My mind is still blown about it actually. To have other people understand you completely without judgment is why we are on this earth. It is why we have bonds and how we survive.

The myth from most people is that the addict needs help, not the family unit. And this was my belief for a long time as well. It was all about him getting better. What most people do not realize, and I did not realize in the beginning, is that the family also needs help. They also need support and recovery along the way. So much happens to the family unit when addiction is present, so much to break it down, so much to fuck up the whole of the unit, that every single person involved gets to seek help to recover. If the addict goes in to recovery but the family does not, chances are they will not understand how to help themselves move forward or how to help the addict move forward.

Me speaking my truth allowed others to do the same, allowed me to have the courage to get therapy, to join an Al-anon group, to join a spouse recovery group and to speak even more about my experience. It allowed me to write this book, which I started without any expectations of someone reading it. It started with me just getting down on paper my experience.

Sharing our truth and getting help is so powerful and necessary to recovery outside of the addict getting help. There is so much complexity to the family unit during recovery. We get to learn how to move forward, how to forgive, how to lean on another and how to know we are not alone and to have support. We get to understand this is also about us, and what we need to do so we can live a happy and fulfilled life regardless of our loved one's actions and decisions. We get to learn detachment from the outcomes and learn how to be peaceful. We also get to learn how to create a safe space for our loved one, but also for ourselves.

I was able to learn how to communicate in a loving way, and what to do for myself in the case he drinks again. The last time he drank heavily, I was able to go sleep in the other room, avoid yelling and screaming and fighting and be at peace in my own mind. I realized in that moment that no matter what, I was going to be okay. Me. I was going to be fine regardless of what he was doing or going to do. I was no longer going to argue with a drunk person, I was no longer going to try to control what did he, and I was no longer going to rub it in that I knew what he was doing. I was simply giving myself permission to just be me and do what I needed to do for myself. I would never have learned all of this had I not gone through my own recovery process. I would never have grown in to the person I am without all of the systems I took on to get help and make myself better. I wouldn't be the person I am now had I not gotten help and stopped hiding out. Come out of hiding. I am here for you, and I will make some coffee and talk with you, or we can go smash something and let some anger out. I will walk with you to an Al-anon meeting, or drive you to therapy. Or just listen without judgment. Either way, whatever you decide to do, please come out of hiding. The world needs your voice. You need your voice. And you deserve recovery for yourself.

Sharing my truth was the best thing I did for myself. It has allowed me to heal, allowed me to connect with others and maybe even help a few people along the way as well. WE are not alone in this, we have much more in common than we have different, and we all get to lean on one another. The truth is, you have no idea what this is like unless you are going through it yourself, and even then, every situation is so different it is still difficult to understand completely. But the more we use our voices and talk about it; the more healing will happen and the less stigma and shame will be able to come to the surface. This is exactly why this book exists and this is exactly why I am breaking my silence on this.

We can break the silence. But we have to start with speaking.

Chapter 8

The simple sound of ice.

I never would have thought something as simple as ice would make me crazy. But here we are. I learned recently that Post Traumatic Stress is something all people can experience based on any type of trauma. I, like so many people, thought PTS was something reserved for soldiers in a war, but this is not the case.

I learned I also deal with post traumatic stress based around the history of my relationship. I honestly put this at the back of my mind for so long thinking I did not go through enough trauma to warrant any sort of lasting issues from it. I was definitely experiencing imposter syndrome to the fullest in this. People grow through serious issues – abuse, war, losing someone. I did not think being married to alcoholic was as bad as trauma others experience. However, we all experience our own trauma in our ways, and no one is less or more than the other, they are just different.

So back to the ice. I had a pretty intense therapy session and we discussed certain things that make my blood boil these days, things I never would have guessed in my life would make me feel the way they did. Hearing ice hitting a glass cup, it makes my blood boil. It makes me nervous. It makes me angry. It makes me start to second guess all the things. Even now, when I know that glass does not contain any alcohol it takes me right back to those moments when it did, and I was upstairs stewing over what was going to happen after hearing those ice cubes hit the glass.

Immediately when I would hear it, I would image how the rest of the day was going to go. Would we get in to a fight, would he have just a couple or would it turn in to an all-nighter? The angriest I would get is when he had already had several and we decided to go to bed and he was pouring himself one last drink for the night. A drink that would usually end up sitting on the nightstand and creating a ring. Or a drink he would sit downstairs and finish alone while I was getting ready for bed alone. The thoughts would run through my head like crazy and I would imagine all of these scenarios of what our life looked like and what was to come. I would start to completely spiral and lose hope.

I have an issue with spiraling thoughts. Once I start, it seems so hard to get them to stop, and my imagination is always much worse than the truth. Something I would always tell my husband – just tell me the truth, because the story I am conjuring up in my brain is probably way worse. So, it would start with me imagining the night, and wanting to say something about that one last drink – or say something about him limiting his intake for the night. That would turn in to me imagining how he would respond, what type of attitude that would lead to for the rest of the evening, if we would go to bed angry, if we would even go to bed together. Man, the thoughts just spun around in my brain.

What I realized in my therapy session was that I certainly have post traumatic stress and it does impact my life by forcing me to relive emotions and the psychological spiral I would go down each time I had a trigger. So, the simple sound of ice hitting a glass was a trigger for me. I have been learning different coping mechanisms to grow and move forward and stop the spiraling, but it is still there and it is Post Traumatic Stress. Diagnosed from a real live psychologist. It is tough to turn away from that kind of evidence and diagnosis. No more imposter syndrome, no more feeling like it couldn't be that bad for me. It was right there in my face and there was something I could do about it.

Once you receive a diagnosis, it can seem super scary, but it is also so freeing and empowering because you now know what is going on and can get the tools you need to move forward and help yourself.

I learned all of my triggers. Driving past a certain place that caused an impact in our relationship – whether good or bad – was still a trigger. Hearing that sound of the ice, even thinking about it starts to make me anxious.

The craziest one was getting sweet messages during the day from my husband. This should be something to celebrate, I know so many people who would love to get the messages I receive from him. They would love to get a sweet video link. But for me, these things occurred after he had about three drinks – yes, I know down to the count, and no, I am not proud of that, but it is part of me now. These would be so sweet and I would immediately start to wonder why he couldn't be this person sober. I started to wonder if it was me, was I just unlovable without some booze in his system? Could he not express how he felt when he was sober because he didn't actually feel that way and he needed alcohol to convince himself he did? Or did it just make him uncomfortable to send it? Oh, the spiraling. Get it now? It gets intense sometimes. Because there is no definitive answer, so the thoughts just keep on coming and get worse usually with each one.

So now when he sends me sweet messages or videos, I have to push back the thoughts that he has been drinking. I have to stop the spiraling from getting out of control and trust that he is on the path he needs to be on, and either way, I am going to be okay. I get to reinforce that no matter what, I am going to be fine. And if he has been drinking that day, I will find out when I get home and we will tackle the handling of that together. So instead of going down the rabbit hole of what is going to happen and how, and how I can control it and all the things, I just have faith and hope that it is going to be alright.

I used to call him right after I received something from him, just to hear his voice. And I would analyze his voice for little sounds that were indicative of his drinking – remember, I knew this person so much better than I once knew myself – I know what drunk him sounds like. I know what a couple of drinks him sounds like. This is not new to me. So I would make up a reason, call him and just listen to his voice. I did not actually typically hear anything he was saying – I was just trying to figure out if I was right. Part of me loves being right, honestly a big part of me loved being right more than anything else –

including his feelings – but on this, I wanted nothing more than to be wrong. But once I got it in my head that I was right, well, that was it. I was on a mission to prove it no matter what that took.

Now, I don't call. I send a sweet message right back. Then I hope for the best. And I try really hard not to look for it later. This is all going to take time and my triggers are going to take time to unlearn – and I may never unlearn them, and may always have to work to not allow them to trigger me too hard.

Now I work to actually listen to what he has to say instead of listening to the way his voice sounds. Now, I think of love instead of fear. We can talk more about love and fear later, but love is always the right answer, just remember that.

But the simple things can send you off completely. And I hope that if you are feeling the same way I did, you understand that you are worthy of your feelings. You are worthy of all the things you are feeling, you have been through trauma no matter how small you might think it is, it is still trauma and it still has an impact on your life. I hope that you will get help in this area as well, whether that is a group, therapy, meditation, whatever. I hope that you will ask for and receive help. I hope that you will reach out to someone you trust and let them know what is going on. You do not have to live with this alone, and you can get help and learn coping mechanisms so the spiraling does not take over your life like it did mine for so long.

And trust that over time, this will become easier and you will get better.

Chapter 9

It's heavy

The world alcoholic is heavy. The word wife is also heavy.

When you mix the two – alcoholic's wife – damn, the weight is sometimes crushing.

You see these situations on television and in the movies. The husband is an alcoholic, the wife is supportive and gets him to stop. Or the wife is abused and eventually leaves. Typically, the outcome of these false relationships is either great or really terrible. No in between. We watch these and think we have an understanding of what it is like, of how we would handle something – or the thought that this would never happen to me. I would never put up with that. Yea, me either.

The difference in television and movies and real life is....well, everything. I never thought I would put up with that, and the view being that if he really loved me, if he really wanted to be with me, he would stop for me. Except that is not how this works – well at least not in my case, and if you are going through the same, I would venture to guess it is not in your case either.

I cannot speak from experience here, but loving an alcoholic, I do have some knowns. It is heavy. It is lonely, and full of shame, it is learning to manipulate but not meaning to.

As I am writing this chapter, I am angry, and my heart feels heavy. Another fight, another round of yelling (which I was working really hard not to do) and another night of frustration and a day to follow that feels...well, heavy. Heavy with pain and that feeling in your stomach, you know, the one. It feels close to nauseated but not quite, a little like heartburn in your throat. Feel me?

The arguments and fights that come along with these issues are insane. An alcoholic is a manipulator, they have had to be, and they do not mean to be all at the same time. The argument of the night came after I asked if he had been drinking, and the answer was no. The answer is always no, even when it should be yes. Even when there is alcohol hidden somewhere in the house, the answer is always no. This is a training that happened, I was trained to disbelieve my husband even if he was telling the truth, because he taught me he would always lie no matter the circumstance. So, when I see the signs and the answer is no, I try hard not to react, but sometimes the reality is, it isn't that easy and realistic to not react. The emotions take over and that is what happened.

The other issue on the table was my issues. It seems like the only time he seemed to care or suggest talking about my own issues is when the arrow was pointed at him and he needed to get it back on me – que the manipulative side. The arguments turn to my faults and of course I get upset. Anyone would get upset when told their own faults, but this was made worse by the fact that he never seemed to want to help me with those faults or support me in any way, only brought them up in an argument or discussion about his drinking, which to me, meant he really did not actually care about me, but held on to certain pieces of information in order to use them against me later. Que the blow up.

Yep, I blew up. I did everything I tell people not to do. I yelled. I screamed. I cursed a lot. When he asked how he could support me, I yelled how and I am pretty sure it went like this, "You could get your lazy ass off the fucking couch once in a while and do a workout with me." I'm not even ashamed or regretful about that one. But I should have said it in a different way instead of screeching it out of my lungs at him. I would have said it to him. But hey, coulda shoulda, woulda. I have come to terms with the fact that I most certainly cannot change the past and moving on is the only option I have.

I knew though, the moment he asked, I knew. He would never get his ass of that fucking couch and actually do a workout with me. He wanted to make a point and feel victorious over me in that moment. But it infuriated me and gave me even more of a notion he had been drinking today. I just knew. There are so many signs and I have observed that person more than most things. I know the way his eyes look, the way his face and hands turn red, the way he talks and walks, the super slow movements of his hands across his head, the way he talks out of the right side of his mouth, how he slurs only certain words and how he laughs. All of it and more. I know that person so well and even the smallest sign of him, I just know. That is not my husband, that is not the man I love so much and the man I want to be with. That man is one I am barely attracted to, the one that makes me so angry and makes me feel so unloved and like I am a complete joke. I say it with fierceness in my soul, I hate this person.

Now, that is freaking heavy as hell. I hate that fucking person so much, and I shut down immediately when I see any little sign of him. And I blew up. I am forever working on it.

The funny part is, I had devised a plan in my head that the next time he drinks, I will just give him a hug. I won't say word, I will just hug him so he knows he is loved and supported, no matter what. However, that requires telling the truth, and he only ever told me the truth one time. It also requires me to keep my cool, which is something I am also forever working on.

So, instead of him telling the truth, we fought. And I was made out to be the one with the problems, the one that cannot get over the past, the one that just cannot seem to let anything go and the one he gets to push all the bull shit on so it is no longer on him. And damn, it pissed me off. It always pisses me off, but this time was like a stab in the neck with a spoon. That bad. So, I told him he was deflecting, he told me about some bull shit a week ago that pissed him off, I told him he gets to learn how to express that in the moment instead of later, he told me how wrong I was and all about my problems, I told him I can't do it anymore – something I have said more times than I like to admit – and then informed him I would be sleeping in the guest room because I needed distance (something I have always threatened to do but have never actually done).

And damn, I pulled my back a few days prior to this and that fucking bed did me in. Talk about pain. Yuck. But a small price to pay to prove a point and to make myself feel better and create distance to eventually make the entire situation better. Which it did.

So, I slept in the other room. And we said goodbye before work this morning, and here I am writing this chapter. Maybe I should've waited until I was slightly more numb, but whatever, I want to be as honest as possible in this as I can. And the fact that I sit at work with a smile on my face and talk with people is almost as bad as the fighting itself, so if I get to be honest here, well then, my day is happier.

The heaviest part about all of this is my drive home. I want to be in my home, but I don't want to go home. Been there? Hopefully I am not alone, but I also kind of hope I am. It is so difficult to not know what I am going to be walking in to when I walk in that door. Will he be happy or depressed? Sleeping off a buzz or tired? In a shitty mood because he did drink, or maybe because he didn't. It is always a crap shoot and always no fair. It is not fair that I made have had a rough day, yet I do not know what I am walking in to when I come home that day. But hey, it's where we are, and I will be headed home shortly and will see.

I am actually proud of myself for taking some space and making sure I was alright first, it has been something I have been working on for a long time and felt good to put it to practice. It was not a mean statement or a fuck you, it was a I need distance from you tonight and I am proud of myself for giving that to me. Detachment is also something I have been working hard on and to be able to detach, sleep in another room while pissed off but still laugh at the show on television was a solid move forward. At least in my book.

The heaviness of having an alcoholic or addict in your life is not something that is easily describable, the pain and anger is real. The lack of support is insanely real. There is a serious lack of support, other than therapy and al anon, both great resources and something that should be in the routine of helpfulness. However, the support goes to the alcoholic, because that is where it is needed, the loved ones get looked over somewhat, they are not the ones with the problem, so they do not need the help and support.

But the truth here is that loved ones also must go through recovery, to get to the other side of whatever side they are currently on. Right now, my recovery consists of therapy, Al anon meetings – ones that are productive, meditation, exercise, time with my dogs, time alone, showers, I could go on and on.

I try to make as much as possible therapy for me. I make a shower therapy, and let the water wash away the day. I make breathing therapy and breathe away the problems and attempt to breathe in the good. I take walks and smell the flowers and look for all the beauty. I take every change I get to make every single thing a piece of therapy for me. I practice being patient and kind when at work and in a frustrating situation, I practice understanding others when they seem difficult. I practice a smile when I want to do nothing of the sort. All of this together relieves the heaviness, even temporarily. Even for the smallest period of time it makes the heaviness go away and allows me to be a better human all around.

The amazing part in all of this is if you work at bettering yourself, it will not only allow you to be a better support, a better partner, but it will turn you in to a better human all the way around. Not that I want anyone else to go through this, however, I know others do, and there is an opportunity here to become a better human in all ways, if you work at it.

When you work on yourself, your perspective changes as well, your mindset. You start to see the beauty in life rather than the ugly. You start to see kindness and love in others, and in yourself.

Trust me, I know all of this sounds fluffy and it is a lot easier said than done. But it is a muscle and if you work at it, it becomes easier to just see the good.

And we get to work together through all of it. There is so much power in speaking your truth, and when you do, not only does your heaviness lighten, but you may just lighten the load for someone else also. Sharing what you are going through might give someone else the courage to stand in their truth and their voice, and no longer go through it alone. This is true for spouses of addiction and any other hard thing in life. You will be surprised to find out how many people carry the same heaviness silently. We get to step out and break the silence, stand together and support one another.

The heaviness does not have to be so heavy. The words do not have to be so heavy.

Chapter 10
It's all about you.

If you spent some time in the 90's you know what song this just brought to my mind. Good old Tupac. And if you don't know what I am referencing, I am not sure about you. I kid, I am sure you are an okay human. Also, I went through a phase of my childhood I truly thought I was so freaking cool and listened to nothing but rap music, and well, I am just so sorry parents. But if that shit comes on now, you better believe I will be jamming out. No shame, I am actually pretty proud of it.

One of the toughest things about loving an addict is there is not a ton of support on our end. The spouses, the family members and loved ones. Yes, we have Al-anon and some other resources, but everything is about them, their recovery, what they need and the progress they have made. We kind of fall to the side and are silent about any struggles or successes we have had in the process. We go through our own recovery and therapy and fight and climb back up to the top. We deal with the tough battle of getting that trust back and losing the anxieties around it. Yet there is no recognition for that and very little support.

I was the one that sat at the hospital several times for the nurses and doctors to tell my husband he was dehydrated and having anxiety. I was the one who put up with the nights that were not so pretty, I was the one who sat with him while he talked about how this was the last time, how he was going to get better and he was on the right track. I listened while he cried about how stressed he had been and that he knew he had to get better. I sat at home while he was in detox and tried to figure out what our family structure was going to be. I was the one who cried and felt terrible about what he was doing. I was the one sitting at home worried to death when he left after a fight and was waiting for some sort of horrible phone call that he had been in an accident. I was the one who nursed him back to feeling better when he was detoxing or hungover. I was patient when he did not want to do an activity because it didn't involve alcohol. I was the one who went to the friend's house when I really didn't want to and stayed much later than I wanted so he could have a good time. I was the one who made excuses when he wasn't feeling well. I was the one who took over on holidays because he was in bed. I was the one who was constantly stressed and worried and working toward something better.

I know you know this story. I know you understand it. We are the silent ones, the ones who sit back and do the work and do all we can to keep up the hope, and make sure everything is ok and attempt to keep the peace. We are the warriors who keep it all together. And it is fucking exhausting.

Especially when the question is, how is he doing today? How is everything going with him? Honestly it is so fucking frustrating and started to make me so angry that so many people stopped asking how I was doing, stopped wondering if I was okay or even realizing that I might not be okay because of all of this. Yes, his recovery is so important and without that we would not be together, our marriage would have crumbled by now if he had not gotten in to recovery. However, it is exhausting to always discuss someone else and never get the recognition for what you do, or even get asked if you are doing alright.

I remember one time, a family member who shall remain anonymous – you know who you are and I know you did not mean any harm with this at all – was talking with me after thanksgiving one year. My husband had drank excessively the week leading up to my favorite holiday of the year. I cook for the whole family and thoroughly enjoy every moment of it. This particular year, I did it all on my own. He was incredibly sick and probably detoxing and upstairs in bed. I prepped and cooked the entire meal, and when family arrived, typically he would let them in and get them something to drink so I could continue. This year though, I did it all on my own. I entertained the family, cooked the meal, served it and cleaned up after. I also made excuses as to why he wasn't feeling well. After everyone left, I was left completely exhausted, mentally and physically. Well, I was having a conversation and finally told my family member why my husband spent most of the evening upstairs. I was totally understanding and trying to be helpful to him, and to the whole family. The particular family member told me to remember that he is getting better, make sure to take care of him and be supportive. It cannot be easy for him to go through this. Now, while I agree, I was furious. I actually think I hung up the phone in a huff.

Yes, I understand this is hard on him. However, I got zero recognition for all the work I had put in that day – completely alone. Without any help from my partner and on top of that taking care of him as well and making excuses. I was so pissed because this is typical of what we go through here. I put in all of this work and the focus was still on him and the demons he is battling. It seemed like no matter what I did, no matter the work or how much I tried, I was never going to get support or encouragement because that had to be saved for him.

It was so fucking lonely for so long. Feeling like I had to fight a battle, keep up the house and the front of happiness, the work, the family, all of it without any sort of support. And we do not even have children, I honestly couldn't imagine this with children and if that is where you are, you are my fucking hero.

All of this is the main reason this book exists. It is the main reason I wanted to write more about what I have gone through, so that we are no longer alone. Because we are not. We get to support each other; we get to make sure we do not feel alone anymore. We get to make sure we have a pack together and support and encourage one another. It is so damn important, because as hard as this is for the addict, it is truly the hardest path I have ever walked. Made even harder by not having much support. It pisses me off honestly, it pisses me off to the point I want every single person going through this know they are not alone, and that I will help you fight for you. And I want every person to know that no matter what you will be okay.

We stay in the silence for so many reasons, but I think mostly because we do not feel like we would have support if we spoke our truth, out of fear of being judged and being outcasted and shamed. And I am done with the silence because it does nothing for anyone. It actually probably makes the situation worse, I am not sure, but it definitely feels that way. We get to be there for one another, because unless you have been in these shoes, you really have no idea what it feels like and looks like. Even so, it is tough to know what that looks like for someone else, because everyone's situations are all so different.

And if you are someone who knows someone who is going through this, call and ask them how they are, not how their spouse or family member is. How they are, what they are up to, what they are working on that they are excited about. Maybe ask them when you could get together with them and plan something that doesn't involve alcohol, because they probably don't want to deal with those feelings when they are trying to relax. Make sure they know you care about them, and make it a little less about the addict in their lives when you talk to them. Let them know they have a safe space with you should they ever need it. Let them know you are there for them regardless of what else is going on in their lives. It is so damn lonely to be in these shoes, maybe just try to make it less that way so they feel like they are a person and have feelings.

The hardest part is we are made to be the solid ones, the ones that keep it together and don't have feelings, but damn. We need help too; we need to know we have people who care about us as well. And it is so damn tough, mainly for me because I did not want to seem selfish. It is anything but selfish to just need another person to be there. It is anything but selfish to ask for help.

Chapter 11

Tricky little Trust.

This speech is my recital, I think it's very vital.

The song was in my head once I typed out the title, and I mean, it fits, so it stays. And now it is currently playing the background as my husband makes dinner and is probably wondering why the hell that was my song of choice. Go with it, babe, now you know.

Trust plays such a vital role in relationships, it is odd because it is easy to lose, and super hard to get back, and even harder to maintain once it returns. And the craziest part of all, is at the end of the day, it is your choice, trust. You get to choose to trust or not based on whatever that means for you. So, it is not something you can look to, or ask someone else for. We agree trust is huge, but most people are slow to agree that it is under our control.

Well, the things my husband did cause the loss of trust, yes. Lying will always cause a loss of trust in a relationship, especially one where friendship is the base. We have to be able to lean on the people we love, be vulnerable with them and let those walls down if we want the relationship to move forward at all. So, in a marriage, or close friendship, trust is of the utmost importance.

In our marriage, he caused the majority of the trust lost. He lied about alcohol, he lied about women – in the very beginning, not since – and this caused me to question his behaviors going forward. It seemed for a couple of years, I would work my ass off to trust him again and then bam! He would do something else, or repeat an old behavior and we were back to square one. And I started the work all over again, and it didn't seem like he put much work in to it at all. It felt so unfair, but in all honesty, he was putting work in to it, I just did not want to see it because it allowed me to be the victim for so long. Allowing yourself to be the victim is so much easier than admitting any fault or admitting someone else is actually putting in work. It is just so much easier. And honestly, you get a little more attention, granted it is not healthy attention, but attention nonetheless. Not easy to admit, but hey, it's the truth. And I am working on allowing more of that tricky little bastard in to my life.

So, he lied, but here's the hard part, I allowed it. Each and every time I would end up forgiving him, end up listening to what he had to say and agree to move on. He couldn't grasp why, when it happened again, that my trust level went right back to zero. Actually, it probably metered in to the negative if that is possible. Once trust is broken, it goes right back to empty, that is the hard part for others to understand, and it was definitely hard for him to understand. It happened again, he lied again, but how is that related to the past? Well, because honesty is honesty, and lies are lies, once they happen consistently, it is difficult to believe they won't happen again, and that wall put up gets taller and taller. The more this happens, the more difficult it is to have a healthy relationship with someone. You are always expecting them to lie, and they know you are going to get mad either way, so why tell the truth when either way, you are going to flip out? It never made sense to me, but it does now.

If I am going to be angry, why not lie and hope for the best – me not being angry – than tell the truth and get the anger over with. What he didn't understand back then was the more he would tell the truth, the more that wall would come down, the more trust was built, regardless of how mad I was about the truth, trust would start to come back. Over time, and a ton of therapy, I was able to truly express what this would mean for us. If he continued to build up that trust, tell the truth and deal with it right then and there, we would be able to move forward and the past honestly wouldn't matter anymore. This is all way easier said than done and has taken a very long time to get where we are, and we are still working to move forward, but slowly and surely the trust is coming back to our relationship. This is where I get to say the previous forgiveness was worth it to be where we are. But it took a long time and a lot of work from both of us.

The last time he drank, of course I knew, we were leaving for a trip. A trip where I would get on stage and talk about being the wife of an alcoholic, nothing more real than that, huh? I got home from work and realized he was drunk. He told me I was crazy, and that he had not been drinking, which I knew was completely false. As I have mentioned, I am not proud of it, but

I know that version of him so well, for a while I knew that person better than I knew myself. I was immediately deflated. I was giving up so much hope. But I sat with him in the garage, and explained to him there is no room for shame in our marriage. There is no room for lies anymore either, this was it. He needed to be honest and equally I needed to allow him the safe space to be honest. He admitted everything, he told me everything and explained how he was feeling. Now, I am not going to sit here and pretend I kept my shit together and didn't blow up on him. I did. Momentarily, and then quickly remembered that gets us nowhere and I was only making a tough situation tougher. I told him I did not want him on this trip, and yelled. Again, it takes a lot of work. But I got it together quickly.

Here's the thing with trust, it is a two-way street. He has to have the courage and strength to tell me the truth regardless of what that means, and I equally get to make a safe space for him to do so. I am not putting fault on anyone here, but how would it feel if you told the truth and were still admonished for it? You really would be hesitant to tell the truth in the future. A lie would sound so easy, and so much better than the truth, especially if the other party never found out about it. I was not creating a safe space for him to be honest. He was rarely honest in regards to alcohol, but in the moments he was, I was not responding to his honesty, I was reacting to it. I would yell and scream and be hateful toward him, and remind him over and over how I knew the whole time and was waiting for him to be honest. It was like a badge of honor that I was right, and instead of giving him some sort of credit for telling me the truth, my ego took over and I just had to rub it in that I was right instead.

The funny part in all of this – funny strange not funny haha – is that I always did know. And if you know as well, understand no matter what is said, the truth will always come out, it will always show its face. No matter what it will prevail, so right now, in this moment, you don't have to be right. And you certainly don't have to rub it in that you are. The truth will be there for you, always, but right now, you can let it lie. Yes, I wrote that on purpose.

I know now to be there for him. To let him know I was appreciative of him telling the truth. This did not mean I forgot about it, or I wasn't allowed to be disappointed and upset, but I got to respond and show that in a loving way. Yes, you can still show disappointment and hurt in a loving way, you can explain your feelings instead of screaming them at someone, novel idea isn't it? I could still provide him a safe space so he knew when he did tell me the truth, I was going to be there for him.

Something so interesting and hard to wrap my head around was a statement from therapist. He said to me, maybe he just cannot tell you the truth right now. What?! That was so hard to understand. How could I possibly have the compassion in my heart to understand he couldn't tell me the truth? How could I wrap around the idea that lying was alright? That is ridiculous. Or is it? Once I meditated on that thought for a moment it actually cleared my mind quite a bit. What if that's all it was. What if I dropped the pressure of everything and stopped being such a perfectionist and pushing that ideal on him? What if I stopped thinking about what I would do and start to contemplate how hard this must be on him? What if I did all of these things instead of constantly berating him about telling the truth and just let it be what it is? This is when a book came in to my life that changed my life. It talked all about detachment and how loving that can be. It showed me that his decisions with his life are his and mine are mine and we can coexist in that without pushing what we want for ourselves on one another.

When I woke up to this and realized how blissful detachment is, I started to understand just how much I was projecting my expectations for myself on my husband. I started to understand how much I projected my expectations for myself on everyone in my life. Especially when I wasn't living up to my own expectations, that meant I could project on others because I wasn't happy with myself. Sounds like I was dream, right.

So, if I could just stop drinking, I should expect that of him. If I could make up my mind to make something happen, he should too. If I was perfectionist pain in the ass, he had to be one as well. If I needed to get something done, he was expected to also get just as much accomplished. He wanted to lie on the couch? No fucking way, dude. We have things to do, when in actuality, I had things to do, I was just jealous he was able to relax. I was never able to relax so how could anyone else? What a painful way to live for both of us, for anyone that had the expectation list in my life.

Here is my takeaway from this portion of my life and experience, our expectations of ourselves have nothing to do with anyone else. Other's expectations of themselves are really none of our business, even if that person is our spouse or family member. I was so busy expecting my husband to be just like me I forgot he is his own person and has his own things to work on and towards. I forgot to work on myself at all, and made his productivity my entire life. I got angry and resentful because he would drink, because my expectation was he shouldn't and he could stop if he really wanted to. I was frustrated when he wouldn't do something I expected of him.

My step mom said it best to me once when I told her, I don't expect much. She said, "how about just the first three words instead?" I don't expect. What a revelation. I practice that now, as hard as I can, and of course, it is not perfect, but it makes it a lot easier for me to just try not to have expectations out of other people, and not to define myself by other's expectations of me.

And maybe someone just isn't in the right frame of mind to tell you the truth right now. Maybe they are not directly lying to you, but just cannot muster up that courage and strength right now. Is that really that bad? Maybe it is for you, maybe you, like me when I first heard it, cannot wrap your head around such a strange theory of thought. Maybe you need to meditate on it a bit as well. It's just not the time someone can tell the truth. That's it. No drama, no screaming and yelling, it just is what it is right now, and my job is to create a safe enough place for others to confide in me and trust me with their truth. Maybe I can work on myself a little bit more to make this the truth. Maybe I can practice more compassion, especially in the times when I don't want to. When it's hardest, maybe I can put in a little more effort.

Now, I know this sounds like I am condoning lying. I am not. It is never okay to lie to those you love. And we have all done it, so come down off your high horse right this second and stand right beside me. I have learned I am allowed to admit my faults, I am allowed to admit when I fucked up, and I am allowed to know that is slowly making me a better person. So, come join me over here. It's a pretty cool space. The pressure is off, you get to enjoy more love in your life — mostly for yourself, and revel in the beautiful moments. I am not saying lying is okay, not at all, I am simply saying sometimes you just get to sit in the situation and practice patience that someone else will do the right thing.

We get to admit our faults and acknowledge we are working on becoming a better person. Now, let's allow space for those we love to have the same opportunity.

And keep up a little hope that things are going to turn out exactly as they should.

Chapter 12

Drawing the line in the sand.

In the beginning, when I first realized my husband had more than just an excessive drinking habit, I thought I had drawn a line with him. The first one was don't drink during the week. That was my line, and he followed it for about two weeks after a huge fight, simply to make me happy. Or he showed me the side of him that wasn't drinking during the week anyway.

Next up it was going out – hey could you only have like four tonight? That would be great. That was my next line, and again, he made me believe that yes, that was going to be fine and it never happened.

Then the line of not having any in the car. Yes, he had alcohol in the car – as most of us had in our lives, and I know he is not ashamed of his past and I am not ashamed of it either, so this is the truth, take it or leave it now. I told him no more. It was just plain dumb – to which he would agree with me now. It is never a good choice to have alcohol in your vehicle. So, he stopped doing that for an amount of time as well.

Basically, everything I asked of him, all of the lines I drew were respected for a short amount of time until maybe he thought I had forgotten about them or it wore off and he would start again. To which I would always have something to say, and so would he and we would fight about it. This usually ended with me just letting go of it, or waiting until the next time to say something so that we could go to sleep. I was usually the one who kept us both up because I couldn't let something go, but after a minute, damn a girl needs sleep too and nothing was being accomplished.

Then what I thought was the final line in the sand. I told him to stop. Just fucking stop. It wasn't hard and he had to get help and stop it altogether. I knew it was a problem. I knew he couldn't just slow down, that was not possible for him, and it had to stop. So, I put my foot down for what I thought was the last time. After one argument and fight after another, he reluctantly decided to start going to meetings. To me this looked like progress and I was happy, but to him, it really meant nothing. My line in the sand was him just trying to appease me and wasn't actually doing anything for himself. This is what happens when you draw a line, the person makes decisions based on what you want, not what they want or are ready for. It typically does not work out. And that was the case here. It didn't work out. In fact, he was going to meetings and coming home from them intoxicated, which made me even more furious, even though I was happy he was seeking help in some way or another. And honestly, I am grateful for these meetings either way, because they did eventually get him where he is now. But this was the line in the sand I drew to make myself feel better, which temporarily it did, but it did nothing for him at the time.

Another line. I drew a line St. Patrick's Day weekend. I discussed this already here, but it is worth mentioning again as a note in the lines in sand. I left, that was my line. I was finished, I couldn't handle any more and I decided enough was enough. I drew my line and it was me walking out the door. This led to him choosing detox, which was amazing, but I still was unsure how to feel about that. Proud? Happy? Disappointed? I was all over the place here, but it seemed like the line drawn was appropriate and I was happy I had the courage to stand in my voice. I just hoped this time if was for him and not because I drew an imaginary line in the sand.

Since the time he went to detox, I have drawn so many lines and he has crossed nearly all of them. And we have grown and learned.

Now, my line drawn is how much I will take before I walk away. Now, if he has been drinking, I try to stay as calm as possible and usually just try to walk away and be in my own space by myself. I stay in the spare room and collect my own thoughts. I meditate or just stay silent with myself. Or I stare mindlessly at the television until I fall asleep, whatever gets me there.

This doesn't always happen, because I have a tendency to get super pissed and I have been working on that for years, but time and time again, I get better at making this my reality and really being able to have a positive outlook on our life and the future. It has taken so much practice, this was not something that happened overnight or even over a year. I also got comfortable with a thought that it might not work out. I know that sounds super weird and maybe even a little counterproductive, but getting comfortable with the thought that no matter what I will be okay was something I needed to survive. It was what I needed to make sure I knew I was alright and I could move forward because I have and if I got to the point that I couldn't, I had a plan. I am a planner, so regardless of how it sounds, it made me feel so much better about everything. It is what it is.

The main takeaway here is that lines drawn are not for everyone. The lines I drew, he would cross because I drew the line for him. And I have been very clear that you cannot control any of what someone else does or doesn't do. So me drawing this line for him was counterproductive for him – it was good for me – and therefore it did not work. Once I drew a line that served me, that was about me, for me, was when I was able to finally have some peace and keep a line. Once I made the line something about my behaviors and responses, it made all the more sense for both of us.

If you are drawings lines, make sure they are the right ones. If you are drawing a line that determines their behavior, it is probably the wrong one. If you are drawing a line based on what you will do if something happens, that is going to be the line that no one can cross but you, and the line that determines your behavior.

We can still draw lines in the sand, we just get to make sure they are the ones that are going to be productive for us, no one else.

Chapter 13

This has nothing to do with you.

What a tough concept to attempt to understand. I get it, I was there too. It was so hard for me to understand how this had nothing to do with me. I was directly involved. I felt like certain things I would do would trigger behaviors or keep him from drinking. How could this not be about me? Well, because it wasn't, and it isn't.

Addiction will never be about anyone but the addict. Nothing we say or do will make the person stop, or give them a reason to continue, no matter what might be said during a heated argument. There is nothing we can do to control someone else. Especially when addiction is involved, no matter how hard we try. Trust me, I really freaking tried. And I drove myself crazy.

When I first heard the phrase, this has nothing to do with you, I was super offended. How dare someone else tell me about my relationship, about what I am going through, about what I am able to do and what is about me. Then, when I truly started to understand what that meant, it felt really freeing and empowering. I cannot control it, I cannot change it, what a feeling. I can do nothing to make this better or worse, so I was free. I was free from trying to do so anymore. It really felt great and I felt silly for being offended by it. But it is seriously tough to grasp, especially when you are knee deep in the situation.

I have done so much research, read so many reports and articles, gone to so many meetings, I was trying to control it, remember? I did everything I could. And from what I can gather, addiction is in the brain, it is basically a chemical imbalance. Do you really think you can do something about a chemical imbalance? Do you think you can control that in someone else's brain? Hell, we have a hard-enough time just trying to control our own brains, let alone trying to do that for someone else. No thank you. Life is hard enough already, why make it that much harder by attempting to do the impossible? I don't know, but I certainly tried for a long time.

The addict is the only one who can do the work, put in the effort and make a change for themselves, and in case you haven't caught on to how important this is, there is absolutely nothing you can do about that. This is not about you. It is about them. It is about the effort they put in to get well. It is about the recovery they do for themselves, and that unfortunately has nothing to do with you. Sounds like a selfish statement, but really, it just frees you up to allow you to work more on yourself and your own recovery. It allows you to let go, detach and truly put the work in elsewhere – in the most loving way, of course.

My husband would actually say this to me from time to time. It is not about you. I would get so angry, because I was right there in the argument with him. I had just as much skin in this game, I had put the time in, I had the fights, I went to therapy, I did the work – all the work I possible could. But he was correct. His recovery and addiction had nothing to do with me. It was his program, his work, his problem, his addiction. Mine was mine. And my recovery and work had nothing to do with him. The two are separate and honestly, they have to be in order for either of you to get well.

It is not about you. It is about them. Your recovery is about you, theirs is about them. You are more likely to get well when you focus on yourself, your relationship with yourself, your own self-love (shameless plug for my last book, The Expedition, go getcha some). You will be more successful for yourself and in your relationship when you are in a better space for yourself than you ever will if you are enthralled and too involved in their recovery. This is something I am incredibly grateful to have found. I was so consumed with what he was doing always, and how much he drank and what his behavior looked like, I forgot about myself most of the time. I lost touch with who I was and what I wanted from the world and how I wanted to impact the world. I completely lost myself, and that is 100% on me. I chose each time to be more involved with him and his recovery than to do anything for myself. This was the opposite of what I needed to be doing, I just had no idea at the time. I didn't realize until I actually started to get help.

There has to be mutual work on any relationship, but when recovery is involved, whether as the alcoholic or the spouse or family, that recovery gets to be separate experience and work.

This has nothing to do with you, and that is so fucking empowering. Let it be.

Chapter 14

Judgey McJudgerson

You are not exempt from this one, and neither am I. We have all been there, hell, sometimes I still catch myself being super judgmental. It's all bull shit. It is so easy to judge something from the outside, not knowing anything about what it means or how it feels. It is easy to sit back and judge an addict's behavior when you have zero understanding of what it actually means to be an addict.

In the beginning, I would push my husband to just stop drinking, just cut it out, it cannot be that hard. And every time he drank, my judgement went crazy. He chose it, every single time. He chose it over me, over anything in his life. And I would berate him and tell him he should just stop it. Then I learned. I took on some research, and so did he. I will not talk about his reasoning, because it is his story to tell – that is a line I will not cross.

What I will talk about is the actual reality of alcoholism. Alcoholics cannot just stop. Let me enlighten you on what happens when an alcoholic stops drinking. They end up in the hospital. They can end up with seizures, and heart attacks and panic attacks and all sorts of really ugly things. The truth is, they can die. And from what I understand, I am no expert, alcohol is the only substance that can actually kill you on withdrawal. And they are no easy thing – withdrawals. It is ugly, it is a mess and that is the reality. It is extremely dangerous to just quit drinking for an alcoholic. It really should be medically monitored. Again, I am not a professional here, but if you count experience as expertise, then maybe I just am.

The reality that so few people see. The reality that family and friends see all too well, and typically hide from the world. We see that reality and we make our own decisions. I decided alcohol was no longer necessary in my life, and that judgment I felt was tough.

Alcohol is so present in our lives, with our friends and family and it is so normalized that no one takes a moment to think about the actual consequences of too much alcohol use. It is in every store, on the shelves, present for anyone. And those that have to walk past it, and stop for a moment to make a decision that could completely change the course of their lives, they are shamed and judged for it.

From the outside, there are so many fucking opinions. It is exhausting. So many people telling you what you should or shouldn't do. How to live your life. When I first stopped drinking, those few who knew about my husband's history would talk to me all about what I should be doing, and telling me how I needed to just live my life. Well, I was, and alcohol was no longer a part of that. Que all the damn judgments. They were everywhere.

The same judgements when I would ask my husband to get help and he wouldn't. Or ask him to please stop and he wouldn't. The ugly reality hit me every single time, that I was the same time of judgmental.

So much judgment. My message here would be to beg everyone to just not judge other people's lives and decisions. It might run much deeper than you could ever imagine.

And when people are sensitive about something, maybe just leave it alone. I bet it definitely runs much deeper than you could ever imagine.

Chapter 15

Hey, Jealousy

The Gin Blossoms are one of my favorite bands on earth. And Hey, Jealousy is my absolute favorite song. There is no real reason why, I just love the rhythm, the lyrics and Robin Wilson's voice belts out the tune in such a perfect way.

I never really thought about the words until I was dealing with a situation of real jealousy. It takes a lot for me to be jealous or envious. These are not common emotions for me, so when I do feel them it feels so foreign, so strange, and I struggle with how to handle it.

We had decided to take my mother in law down to the Las Vegas strip and check out the giant Christmas tree out front of T Mobile arena. It was supposed to be amazing and I saw posts on social media of it going up. Christmas is my favorite time of year, I know, so unique. We drove down, found a parking spot – if you don't know why people who live in Las Vegas rarely go to the strip, these are two of the most common reasons why – and walked over to see the delightful tree. Only to find out that it would be two more weeks until they actually lit it. Great. But we decided to make the best of it and wander around the area around the arena. There are several little restaurants and shops along the walkway there, and a nice fountain, I am a sucker for beautiful water fountains.

We were standing outside of a bar, Chad decided to go in and him and his mom got a drink, this was obviously prior to the recovery days. These were the days when we knew there was a problem but he thought he could get it under control himself and did not think it was much of an issue. Those days. I opted to not indulge in this anyway and not have a drink that night. I am not sure, I think this was the beginning of me becoming hateful over alcohol, the beginning of me wanting nothing to do with it. Or I just was pissed he was having a drink, who knows. Either way, I walked to sit outside and wait for them. I wanted him to know I was pissed, but did not want his mom to know I was pissed. God forbid someone else knew I was pissed at my husband, as if that never happens with couples.

As I sat outside, I was watching a group of people inside the bar. It was one of those bars that has the open area on one end, so it is inside but like you are also sitting outside. I love those bars. Anyhow, I was watching this group of friends, they were all laughing and enjoying one another. One of them yelled something and they all started laughing hysterically. They were celebrating the Vegas Golden Knights win and had obviously just come from the game and were in amazing spirits. I just sat and watched them. Drinking their beer, the waitress brought over shots and they all toasted one another and took the shot together. They laughed, talked, shared, danced, they were having such a great time.

I was jealous. It was overwhelming.

I walked back in to the bar to find Chad and his mom ordering their drinks and chatting with two girls, who I found out were from Canada and were having a blast celebrating in this city a sport they were familiar with and loved. They were joking and laughing and chatting up my husband and his mom, and he was chatting them up as well. Don't worry here, I don't. He has never had any intentions of doing anything inappropriate with another woman, that I am secure in and I have never worried about it. Plus, his mom would kill him, of that I am more certain than anything.

But I was jealous. And not that he was talking up other women. Not that they were having a great time with him. I was envious that they had no idea what was under the surface. They were me years ago, talking up this awesome guy having no clue what was coming. I was envious I didn't have that anymore; all the secrets and issues and bad feelings had come to the surface and our relationship was falling apart because of it. I felt awful we were not there anymore and all of this had bubbled up, I felt horrible I had the feelings I did about my husband. I felt anger toward him, and resentment, and these ladies were able to have a good time because all of that wasn't up there on the surface. I wanted to be back there so badly. I wanted to go back to that and be the blind person I once was before all the issues came up. I felt like I could scream with the envy I was feeling there. I am sure I was not the nicest and most talkative person that night, only feeding in to what I was feeling and honestly making it worse.

I was jealous of the group of friends laughing and having a good time and drinking. I was jealous they could drink together. I was jealous anyone could drink at all and it wasn't an issue. They were able to have a fun night out, enjoy each other and alcohol and not have an issue when they woke up in the morning. They could have a blast together, and not have to wake up in the morning wondering if their partner was going to sneak off to the gas station to get a drink because they couldn't function without one. They didn't have to worry about him insisting on driving home even though I knew it is the worst idea. They are not going to have to worry about the fight that is coming because alcohol is an ever present and growing issue in your life. Maybe they do worry about all of these things, but in that moment, it did not seem like they did and that made me feel jealous of all of them. I just watched and wanted to just sit there and cry. I wanted to go back to the days I could go out, even go out with my husband, and not worry about a thing. To wake up in the morning, maybe feel a little crappy and go on about my day, not thinking about alcohol for another week.

I was jealous that alcohol and the thought of it, and the thought my husband's growing problem was so present in my mind that I thought about alcohol every single day. Sometimes all day. These people didn't have to think about that. They didn't have to think about the repercussions of what alcohol does to the body, how it makes your partner in life look tired and cranky, how it makes him not want to do anything with you, not want to move really. How your life has been wrapped around where the next one is. How travel plans turn in to where he can get a drink and when, and when the next one will be after that. Want to go hiking? Nope, there is no alcohol there. Want to go to this place? Nope, they don't serve alcohol. How every minute of the day is surrounded by this substance. So much that you start to hate it. Except when you come across people enjoying it like you used to.

I was jealous. And I didn't cry, because you know, public places. But I really wanted to. I really wanted to cry and scream at him that I hated him for taking away a part of my life I never even thought about. I wanted to get a cab home so I didn't have to be with him much more, and to see if he would notice I left. How long it would take him. Because at that point, it really seemed like alcohol was his number one, and I went unnoticed for the most part. So how long would it take? I wanted to tell his mom I was leaving and this was the reason why. I wanted to explain to her just how much this had impacted our lives. But I didn't. I walked back outside and stood out there watching the people, wanting to cry and waiting for my husband and mother in law to come back out so I could pretend I was fine. I know I didn't do a great job at that pretending but he never seemed to notice at that time.

This was when I really started to hate alcohol, when I really realized there was a problem and when I also realized I never thought this would be my life and if I really wanted it to be my life. This was the start of so much thinking in my life, mostly of whether or not I could this. He had yet to admit this was as big a problem as it was, and I had no idea if I could handle it or if I wanted to. This night made a huge impact on my thought process and I will remember it for my entire life. That night I was jealous of people doing something as simple as having fun and enjoying alcohol. This was the first night my life really changed because of all this.

The past is gone but something might be found to take its place.

Chapter 16

Guilt

You suck too, but don't let the guilt kill you.

Did you know guilt can actually kill you? It gets in your brain, causes stress and eats away at it until you are stuck in a bed braindead from guilt and stress.

I am not sure if that is 100% true, but damn, doesn't it feel like it sometimes? The guilt has completely eaten at me, and I did not think I would survive it fully. It has gotten that bad. And then I stress about all the guilt, and feel guilty about the stress and round and round we go. That's a sick carousel no one wants to be on but I also know I am not alone on the ride.

The guilt I felt from holding in my emotions was bad. The guilt I felt for not being enough to make him change was worse. Worst of all was the guilt I felt for berating my husband and making him feel any less than what he was.

Here is the twist in the plot of this story. I wasn't perfect either. I tend to lay in on thick when I talk about all the bad

AMBER HAEHNEL

coming from his direction, however, I retreat when I think about all the bad that came from mine. I was no innocent player in this game. Not in the least.

I suck too. I'd like to go in to major detail about all the little things – and huge things – he did that should have torn our relationship apart, and they are all true and everything he did was awful and happened. However, I like to lean toward not giving up my end of the deal that made this such a shit show.

I tried really hard to be the supportive spouse, and I give myself a shit ton of credit for that. It was always me; I was always the one trying so hard, I was holding us together, I was the one putting in the work and I was always doing that alone. As much I do believe it, that is only about 70% true, and that percentage is biased, so take it for what it is.

I had responsibility in this relationship. I have to own up to my portion of the ugliness, just as much as I have to own up to my contribution to the happiness. I want to say that was in a Tony Robbins presentation, if you are going to credit someone for the bad you have to credit them for the good as well. It's not a one-way street. And I was giving myself far too much credit for the good and far too little credit for the bad. On the opposite end, I gave him all the credit for the bad, and very rarely any for the good, even when he did decide to get sober. The guilt I feel from that day is horrendous, and I am working hard to move on.

Picture this – he decides to go to detox, I am still pissed he ruined the one morning I took off for myself, but happy he finally made the decision. I was still skeptical. Then we sit in the emergency room for almost a full 8 hours, until they give him the information for detox. Cool, I wasted an entire day.

But I was also happy he was going. What a weird feeling. Fast forward to the day he was released and I showed up to pick him up, hugged him and we went home. He told me a little about his experience, but I was so anxious and skeptical, all I could think is he wasn't serious and was only doing this to get me to shut up about it. Which was not the case. And after I realized it, the guilt crept in. So hard. I still feel guilty for the way I received him that day. What a way to come home after being gone, in a detox facility nonetheless.

And even now, when I question him, I feel the guilt creeping in just because I am questioning him. Especially if he gets upset about it. Damn.

But here's the thing with guilt. It will go away, and the questions and behaviors I was having are common with this situation, I was also trying to figure out what to say and do, and whether I should be proud or if that was enabling him. How I should act with him now, what he was thinking, how he was feeling and what I could possibly do to make it easier. But I had no clue. Again, guilt over that as well.

The guilt will start to go away. The most important part here, though, is that you work on forgiving yourself. That is the only way the guilt will start to subside is if you work on learning how to forgive you. And forgiveness of yourself is that hardest thing to do, but it will come if you keep working hard at it. Forgive yourself for all the things you are feeling guilty over, after all, they are in the past, and do your hardest to move forward and keep pressing on. Work on not telling yourself old stories and shut them down when they come up. At the same time you are forgiving yourself, stop doing the things that made you feel guilty in the first place. You can't expect to let go of the guilt if you keep acting in the same way you started feeling guilty for, now can you? Nope. Break the cycle. Forgive yourself and move forward, becoming a better person along the way. Thus, forgiveness will happen naturally. Keep working, it gets easier I promise.

Allow yourself space if you need it. Space to think and reflect on your behaviors and the change you want to make in yourself.

And finally, be patient with yourself. You are human and shit happens and it takes a long time to unlearn behaviors and retrain your brain to new behaviors. Forgive and be patient with yourself. The guilt will start to fade, I promise.

Chapter 17

Old Yeller was a dog

Oh man am I a yeller. I am working on it, much like most things in my life, it is a work in progress.

There are two things that really get me going; someone who knows how to push my buttons and does it over and over, and lies. Either of those will get me on a yelling streak and no one wants to be around for that. I am pretty sure my old neighbors felt terrible for my husband and thought I was crazy. I didn't care if the doors and windows were open, if I was in it, I couldn't stop. It made me feel so much better, temporarily. It always made me feel like shit in the long run that I let myself fall apart like that, and then I would relive every second in my head over and over, making it even worse.

I am super hard on other people, but I am way harder on myself. If people only knew the mind fuck that happens with me. And if you read my previous book, The Expedition, you know I am working hard on not being so hard on myself. Try doing that. It's an interesting situation mentally. But I will continue.

I am working on not being so much of a yeller. My family is super opinionated – well one side of it anyway – and my voice has to be loud to be heard, so I was taught over years that yelling is just something you have to do to be heard at all, whether you were angry or not. It took years to become this way, it is going to take years to un-become this way. I get to continue working on it. Get the theme here? Work.

So, how it impacted my marriage. It was my control factor, if I could be louder, I would win. And I always wanted to win. I always wanted to be right, that's what this came down to, being right and winning. I would yell during a calm argument because I thought it made me heard. I would yell my point, and my opinion at my husband because I thought it would finally be that aha moment where he would hear me and understand. However, the case was opposite. After a ton of therapy, I learned that my husband did not grow up yelling, he was actually pretty calm growing up and his family did not involve yelling. So, when I would yell, he would shut down immediately. He stopped hearing me, he stopped listening, he stopped attempting to even do either.

The way I grew up and the way he grew up were working against each other. I wanted to be heard so I was loud, he didn't like loud so he would shut down. And round and round we went, for so damn long. I am so grateful for therapy and having an open mind to it, and an open mind to changing. It is necessary if you want any relationship in your life to work out for the best.

After realizing that yelling was actually making it so my husband heard nothing from me, I had to learn to retrain myself to not yell so damn often. Hell, I even yelled when I was excited or happy or got passionate about a topic, louder and louder I went. And I got to learn how to calm that down. And really mentally make a shift to understand this was not the way to communicate in my marriage and my husband heard me when I was calm and direct. Take the emotion out of it. Huh?? There was no way I could do that. Except I had to.

I would literally have a physical reaction when I was angry, I think most people do. I could feel the hotness hit my face, and my body would start shaking. My vision would become slightly cloudy and my breathing would become short. My chest and throat would get tight and usually I would also start crying in my anger as well. It is incredible to realize all of these reactions.

I did it all. I read the books, I went to therapy, I practiced meditation, which honestly was the one thing that worked the most. I got to take time for myself and learn how to breathe again. That sounds a little strange, but I really wasn't sure how to breathe in order to calm my brain and take a moment to respond. On top of the yelling, I tend to react to most situations. I don't take a lot of time to think about what I am going to say, and I let my hot head take over and do the talking for me. I always, always regret it in the end. I always felt like shit about myself, but I never did the work to stop it. Until this.

I learned the physical triggers of when I was angry. I would feel those physical responses I talked about, and recognize it and say, ok, I am starting to get really angry. Cool. I would take a deep breath to steady my breathing and stop the shortness of breath. I would feel the hotness hit my cheeks and take a step back, out of my head. I made a deal with myself to walk away. Just walk away for ten minutes, it is that easy. You will feel better if you walk away for just ten minutes. And explain that I was getting angry and I needed to walk away for just a few minutes. Usually I would come back after those ten minutes, or sometimes thirty minutes, feeling calmer and ready to have a productive conversation I would feel good about after, and that my husband would actually hear and respond to. It was amazing. What a change.

And the more this happened, the easier it was to calm myself down, not yell and not have regrets afterward. And guess what? We would actually have a productive conversation. What a concept. I would've started this years ago, but you only know what you know until you learn more, right.

It is not easy, it really isn't. But making that deal with myself to walk away when I needed to, to communicate that clearly with my husband and clear my mind for a moment was the start of something so productive and healthy for me and my marriage. Once I was able to recognize those triggers, acknowledge them and shut them down, it seemed like this whole world of control of my emotions opened up.

My point once again is, we get to work on ourselves all the time. We get to figure out where we are and what we can do to make things better in our own lives. I was blaming my husband for "making me angry" for so long and blaming all of his problems on why I was so angry all the time, I never took a look in the mirror and figured out what I could do to better the situation. He was the one doing wrong, so everything was on him. Of course, that is how it works, I was doing nothing wrong and he deserved all of my anger. Except he didn't. No one person deserves to the brunt of someone else's anger, no matter what the situation (abuse excluded from this statement – that is an entirely separate issue). What I learned here was I have a ton of issues also, and just because my husband has a big one, doesn't mean mine disappear. What I learned was I am not perfect and I have a lot of work to do.

And more, I have learned that yelling just gets you nowhere. Old Yeller is a dog, and I am not a dog. I am a human and I get to learn how to communicate properly with others, express my concerns, state what I need and keep it calm, cool and collected. It is definitely a work in progress, and I will continue that work for the rest of my life.

Chapter 18

Nagging gets you nowhere.

You are such a nag. I totally blame media – all types of it – for allowing this portrayal of women. Sitcoms, newscasts, movies, stereotypical wives and girlfriends are telling their significant others how everything should be done, asking them to get something done and nothing happening. Even the joke about the guy who says you don't have to ask him every six months, he will get to it. So. Fucking. Frustrating. And yes, I do fancy myself a feminist, though I prefer the term womanist. Even feminist has a weird vibe about it anymore.

I picture that wife on the latest television sitcom who has asked her husband several times to get something done and he is stereotypically watching television in his pajamas and getting frustrated until he finally jumps up and resentfully yells that he will do it now. Picture it, too? I know I am not alone here. I love these shows, they crack me up, but they are creating a version of what relationships look like that is so unhealthy for us to see.

It is so frustrating because it comes into our daily lives, it makes men think this is the truth and it allows women to believe if they say something more than once they are some typical naggy wife. No. You are not. The word nagging should just be eliminated from our vocabulary.

Well, after I write this book because I need it for this chapter.

Yes, I am going to use this annoying word to convey a message for my own book. Totally contradictory, but it gets the point across nicely, so I will accept it from myself.

Nagging really gets you nowhere. Let's talk about what nagging actually means. It means when you continue to berate someone else for something they do, or don't do, or act, or don't act. It is when we go on and on about something we don't appreciate, and put that in the persons face. Yea, if it were someone doing it to me, I would get super annoyed and probably do the exact opposite of what the person wanted just out of principle for myself and I do what I want. So I completely understand other people not wanting to be nagged at. It just pisses me off that it is normally the wife getting the blame. All that said, in my case, it was absolutely me.

Nagging my husband about drinking. And about taking out the trash, helping me with the dogs, getting up with the dogs, hanging the curtains, fixing the faucet, getting the backyard clean, read this book, take this love languages quiz, go here, do that, act this way. That list could go on and on, but the biggest one was the drinking. I repeated myself over and over. Granted this all came from a place of love and growth and wanting both of us to be better people, but damn it came across super bitchy and out of line most of the time.

The majority of the time, I was pissed about his drinking and not wanting to bring it up yet again, I found something else to be angry about and get on him about. I was on his back about everything, and it all stemmed back to drinking. Cause damn, I was so tired of talking about alcohol. I was sick of bitching at him about and I know he was sick of hearing about it. So, I would come up with something else and in the end, it came back to alcohol anyway, and now we were in a full blown fight and again, I was not creating a safe space for either of us to be honest and forthcoming with one another. Neither was he. It was a sick cycle over and over again.

But it got us nowhere. Me going on about all the things he could be doing only made him feel like he wasn't good enough, like he was an insufficient husband, something he said to me in anger several times. He would yell how sorry he was – sarcastically – that he wasn't a better man for me, and that I decided to marry someone who just is such a shitty husband. Again, a ton of therapy helped me realize this was him telling me this hurt him, it was him showing me he needed me to stop berating him constantly and making him feel like he could do nothing correctly. That he couldn't make me happy no matter how hard he tried. I wish I had known then. But we know what we know until we know better, and then we can do better. I was not doing better back then. I am now.

The nagging I was giving him about drinking only made it worse. It made him think no matter what he did, I was still going to be disappointed, no matter how long he had gone in between drinks it wasn't good enough. I would nag him about going to meetings, meetings that really were not working for him at the time, and he would go anyway, having no productivity and feeling worse about himself in the meantime, but he did it. And then I would bitch that it wasn't good enough, he wasn't working the program, he wasn't doing it the way I would do it. And we would get right back on that ride once again. He felt like shit. Nagging for sure was not working. And that is the key there, he wasn't doing things the way I would. Come on.

I was making my husband feel like shit, and honestly, I was making myself feel like shit too. I had these expectations of what things should look like, how they should feel and how we should honor one another. If this wasn't happening exactly the way I thought it should, the nagging and bitching would jump in and guess what? It made me feel like shit. What we focus on multiplies and I was solely focused on what he could be doing, not what I could be doing.

I was reading the books, I was taking the quizzes, I was putting in the effort to make our relationship better and nothing was changing. Actually, it was probably getting worse. I was putting in all this effort to make him change, or make him better. But in reality, I was doing nothing for myself. I was not working on my own frame of thought and mindset. I was really doing all of these things and putting in all this work to find out how I could make him change the way he was. Oh, how I wish I knew then. But had I not put in all of this work I never would've realized the person I truly needed to work on was myself. For the millionth time, I was shown that I cannot change him. And I think it actually sunk in this time.

I am going to type this out one more time just in case someone needs to read it again – you cannot change other people. You can only work on and change yourself.

I made a decision. No more nagging. No more bitching. Instead I would simply ask and then leave it alone. If I wanted something done, I would either take it on myself and maybe ask for some help, or I would ask him to get it done and let it be. If it took him six months, fine. If it took him a day, cool. If he did it right then, awesome. I allowed myself to detach from the outcome. Ask and let it go. And let me tell you what a change this was. Things started getting done. And when they did, I was sure to notice and say thank you. Holy shit, the power of a little thank you. I had no idea. No passive aggressive statements of how long it took him to do it, or how many times I had asked. I just took it in and said thank you. Also, passive aggressiveness is bull shit anyway, and you need to get right over that if it's what you are doing. I could talk about that forever, but let's stay on track here.

Detaching from the outcome was like magic. I let my feelings about it go, and he actually made things happen. I worked on this with everything, from what I would ask of him, to his drinking. I let go. I cannot control anything he does, and if I try, I will absolutely lose my mind. What is the point, he is annoyed and not doing what I want anyway, and now I am annoyed because I cannot control the situation. No one wins.

But with detachment, everyone wins. The pressure is alleviated, and you get to live life in a more relaxed state. That pressure is what could kill a marriage, and to let it go, you can see and feel the relief on both ends. It is the strangest thing to let go and start to see changes in all aspects of a relationship. That whole term hold on loosely? It is true. Be the loving person you need to be and let go of what you cannot control, especially other people. More than getting you nowhere, it will actually set you further behind. You will lose trust, and no one wants to be controlled anyway, it will push you farther away from where you want to be.

I will put in the recommends section some awesome resources for detachment and where you can get some help in that area. It was one of the most liberating things for me, and I am sure my husband as well. It is a strange concept to imagine, the less you attempt to control something, the more it actually works out the way it is supposed to. And the more you can relax your mind and be in a loving state.

Chapter 19

Pressure is for cookers

I really don't get the whole instant pot craze that started a couple of years ago and took over my Pinterest feed with the number of amazing things you can do with them. I had one. I used it once. It terrified me. I was pretty positive it was going to explode and leave me with scars both mental and physical all to make a meatloaf in 15 minutes. This was only further validated by hearing on the news that this exact situation happened to someone. No, thank you.

I digress.

I have a question for you, do you like to feel pressured into something? Do you like when someone puts on the pressure to get you to do something that you are not ready for? Is it fun to feel like you must go somewhere to please someone else? I am betting the answer to all of this is a resounding no.

So, why, do we feel the need to put so much pressure on someone with an addiction, or in recovery, or a loved one to do something we want them to do – even though we know they need to? I felt the need to put the pressure on high every chance I could. I think it made me feel better honestly. I would put the pressure on to get sober, and then to stay sober, and to be accountable for every second of his day with me. I put the pressure on to report back to me on every move he made. He must have felt like he was suffocating in some claustrophobic tube of a life. Actually, I am sure he felt that way, because he would tell me. I rarely listened though, because this was for his own good. So, I thought. Really, it was just making me feel more in control and better about a shitty situation. How selfish.

With all the pressure I was putting on I honestly thought I was making the situation better. You only do what you know until you know better, then you do better. At this point, I didn't know much, and I thought I was doing the right thing. In reality, what I was doing was making my husband feel like absolute shit. Like he couldn't do things on his own. But that was the point, he couldn't, at least in my head.

I put on the pressure not only to stay sober, but to find new friends, to get a sponsor, to go to meetings. To be a better husband, to do more work around the house, to take on more responsibility in the house, and to work harder at his job and not complain about it. Damn, when I write it out, it seems horrible. And it probably was. I don't know how I would deal with having all of that pressure on me. I would fold for sure. So why was I so nonchalant, so demanding, to put the pressure on him?

Because it made me feel better. It made me feel in control in a situation I had no control over. Not having control was a complete foreign concept to me. I had to have it and demanded it of most things in my life. And order, order was so important to me, blame the military raising on that I suppose. I continued this way, completely damaging my marriage and my own brain so much, until I realized I don't have control over this and that just might be alright. I don't have control over what someone else does. I learned this as a whole, not just with my husband and his drinking. I cannot control how he lives his life or the decisions he makes. Sure, I want to be a part of that, but sometimes I am just not. Just like I cannot control anything anyone else does. When I learned the phrase, you cannot control people, places or things I took it in. But when I really appreciated it for what it was and let it wrap around my heart? That is when I truly started to understand and look inside of myself instead of outside.

I cannot control people, places or things. I can control the way I react or response, I can control my attitude and the way I live my life and my own decisions, so I started there. I started learning about how I can detach in the most loving way, and learned I have my own journey in life and he has his and the more we allow one another to go on those journeys – for whatever that means for each of us – the more freedom we have to be ourselves and find the good sides of ourselves. Both alone and for one another. The better I became for myself with no other motives, the better I became for my husband, my family, friends, co-workers, you name it. Key phrase, the better I became for myself with no other motives.

That is the interesting part, we think we need all of these projects, all of these people are the problem, we get to work on them. When that is the opposite of the truth. Any and everything in your life starts with you. How you respond, what your attitude is, how you feel about something, how you behave, how you treat others. It all starts and ends with you.

And keeping the honesty going here, I very rarely fought or felt angry about my husband not doing enough around the house, or not going to meetings or finding the right friends or sponsor. The main reason I felt angry or upset was because of alcohol and his decisions with it. All the other things were just a way to release my anger in a way that seemed more appropriate. Or maybe it was just something that was right there in our faces, something he couldn't deny, something I could prove he did or didn't do, something I could control.

I would get super pissed about the vacuum not working and be shitty with him, because of course that is his fault, right. I was never actually pissed about the vacuum, sure it was frustrating, but that was not the issue, it was just right there and convenient to bitch about that instead of telling him I felt unsafe and insecure in our marriage because he wasn't telling me the truth. I always knew when he had been drinking, but he rarely actually admitted it. So instead of having a normal, adult conversation I would get pissed about the vacuum instead. Why not?

Well, you heard it here, that is just prolonging a conversation, which in turn comes out in a blow up and neither of you is actually listening to the other, it is just yelling and fighting and all over something that has nothing to do with what is actually wrong. Or, it is what is wrong but at that point, you are both so pissed you aren't being respectful or listening. That just gets you nowhere, absolutely no where. It might feel good for a moment or two to get it out, but in the end, no real progress was actually made, and you get to start all over again. The kicker is you are also not learning anything to progress, so it typically just starts the cycle all over again.

It wasn't until I dropped the pressure on him, and myself, that I found the answers. Now, don't get me twisted here, I still revert to this behavior from time to time, it takes a minute to break shitty habits. How funny that I realize that for myself but refuse to acknowledge that it might take an addict a little time to get things right?! More on that later.

I dropped the pressure on me to be perfect for him and dropped the pressure on him to get it all figured out. I dropped the pressure on myself to be everything for everyone else and allowed myself to just be myself and grow within myself. I dropped the pressure I put on him to do this, go there, be that, friend this person, and all the things. I am sure he felt relief even if he doesn't admit it. Man, it felt good to release the pressure. It felt like someone opened my lid and let some air in. I could breathe a little.

It took a ton of practice, like a lot, and still takes it, but releasing the pressure from my life and all I put on him really made me start to see things in a whole different perspective.

And that was the start. One step at a time.

Save the pressure for the instant pot, friend. And if you know any good recipes, send them my way, cause I really don't get the craze. Insert "WHAT?!" yelling here.

Chapter 20

Wet blankets belong in the dryer.

Don't be such a wet blanket. Stop weighing down the fun.

Oh, man. The guilt of feeling like a wet blanket, like I was weighing down the fun. It never ended and it was worse than the opposite of fun. I say all the time, my husband and I had a ton of fun until it wasn't fun anymore. Yes, I partook in the shenanigans, and I loved every moment of it. We were the life of the party together. We seemed to feed off one another.

After time, and once I realized there was a problem lingering, the fun abruptly stopped. I no longer wanted to go out, I always knew how the night would end. I stopped drinking as much when we were out so that I could get us home safely – though he always insisted he could drive, I rarely let him. I say rarely because sometimes there was no arguing, he was completely fine. This all lead me to start realizing just how much of an issue it was. The people we were surrounding ourselves with were never going to help the situation, they were never going to be supportive of him stopping and the more I realized this the angrier I felt. I would sit and basically wait for him to be ready to go. And when I mentioned leaving it was always after this drink. And then after this one. I grew so frustrated. And eventually got the name of wet blanket. I was no fun, and I was always the one that wanted to leave the fun. I was always to blame as to why we had to leave or why we didn't go in the first place. So be it.

See, other people had no clue what we were dealing with because I never said a word and neither did he. So, when he just had to go do this or that, he knew he would get away with having several drinks and I wouldn't say anything in front of anyone. We have never discussed it, but I really believe he did this intentionally so that I wouldn't say anything. At home, I would say something about how many he had or how maybe he should cool it, but in public, in front of other people I rarely said a word, and he knew I wouldn't. I didn't want to embarrass him or demean him in front of anyone, so I kept my mouth shut and was pretty quiet most of the night, making me super approachable to other people I am sure.

I was creating this vision of myself, and honestly, I did not care in the least. No one knew the issues we were facing.

After some time had gone by, I started speaking up, I lost the care of protecting him and keeping our little secret. I would say things about his drinking, which made him angry, which lead to him drinking more, which lead to me being even more annoyed and wanting to go home. Man, I was a pleasure to be around I am sure.

Even after most of the people knew the issues of what was going on, they only said something to me, never to him. They never reached out on how to support him or said anything to him drink after drink. I started to realize who our friends really were and who we needed to be around. But, at the time, he needed to be around his drinking buddies, and therefore, so was I. This made it even more infuriating, because people would approach me about his drinking, 1 – as if I didn't already know and 2- as if I had some sort of control over the situation. It started making me feel like I was some sort of inadequate wife because I couldn't do anything about my husbands' problems. This lie was perpetuated every time someone made a comment to me about him. Eventually I had no desire to go outside of my home. I did not want to deal with him or anyone else for that matter, and I started to distance myself from all of the things. If you were around during the time and noticed I stopped involving myself – sorry not sorry. I was coping and protecting me for once. And my heart was breaking, along with my hope, and I wanted nothing to do with facing people who were going to only talk to me and not him.

That is the funny part. The stigma. We get shit for not drinking, but no one says anything to the person over there drinking too much. No one has the conversation with the person, just the people around the person. But if he wasn't drinking, oh man, the shit storm that would occur and the poking fun would happen. No one takes it upon themselves to be the supportive friend to say, hey man maybe you have had enough. Or hey dude, your wife seems to really want to go home, maybe we should all go. Nope. Just, why aren't you drinking more? Let's take a shot! Let's keep going. I am not sure why this is, but my theory is if you admit someone else might have an issue, and you have the same behaviors, it might mean that you do as well, so let's ignore the issue together. But I will talk shit over here to someone else about you, regardless of how that makes them feel as well. It's maddening and it was maddening. It is crazy making and I felt like I was headed in the crazy direction.

Here's the thing. I felt this way because I cared deeply for him. I wanted him to be better and I wanted him to realize this was no way to live. There is no wet blanket in that. I went from life of the party having fun, to no longer having fun in this and feeling weighed down, but I was not weighing anyone else down. I had to come to terms with what others do is none of my business and what others think of me is none of my business either. I did not want to exist any longer in toxic situations and that was starting to show the more I put myself in those toxic situations. I started to become closed off and cold. I started to realize where I wanted to be, and this was not it.

Realizing what is toxic and pulling yourself away from that is survival mode and is going to do good for you. The people around you don't want you to change or go, so they push against it and wonder why you are changing. They don't want to change, so you cannot either. The more you pull away from that, the healthier you are going to be. And the more room you make for the people who support the changes you are making and the growth you are presenting.

We now have very few friends, very few that stuck around or who don't feel uncomfortable with our not drinking and that is completely ok. The relationships we do have don't feel weighed down – no wet blankets over here – and the toxicity level has dropped dramatically. And it feels wonderful. Of course, we both miss people we had in our daily lives in the past, but we miss a version of them. And here's the thing, in this process, if you do not have supportive people around you, you are not going to be making the best choices for yourself, so we only keep the most supportive people around these days. And we choose to spend our time wisely.

Wet blankets belong in the dryer — and neither of us are wet blankets. Remember that the next time you feel like you are the one weighing down the party.

Chapter 21

You are allowed to be grateful.

I am writing this chapter while crammed on a plane, on a flight to Indianapolis for a convention and family connection. The significance of that is I actually had a ton of anxiety around leaving on this trip. And not for the reasons I had in the past. I used to be the person that would be so stressed about my husband's behavior while I was away, I would not even enjoy the trip or really allow myself to do anything I enjoyed. That is not the case on this trip. And I am tremendously proud of the work I have put in to get to this space. So brag moment.

The case here is I miss him and want him to be along the ride with me. What a change in mindset there. It still kind of blows my mind sometimes when I really think about it. That is where my anxiety is coming from on this trip, that and I hate leaving work. I am working on it.

I have learned something invaluable in this journey with myself and my husband. I am allowed to be grateful. I am allowed to be grateful to something that completely turned my world upside down, completely left me defeated and deflated multiple times, nearly destroyed me and my marriage. I am allowed to be grateful for something that nearly took me down. I am so grateful.

I am not happy about some of the moments of the past, and I do sometimes wish things could be completely different. However, without everything we had gone through, without the growth we forced ourselves to go through, without all the classes, the therapy, the groups, the talks, the fights, we would not be nearly where we are today.

This is all to say there is freaking hope. There is hope, and if you keep remembering that, it will serve you in the long run. There is hope in the hopeless moments. There is hope when you feel like giving up, when you feel like throwing your hands in the air and letting addiction completely rule your life, take over and start over somewhere else. There is still hope, you just might have to look a little harder for it than usual. You might have to look deep in your heart or pull it out of the depths of your soul. And hope is the hardest to find when you truly feel like you have nothing left, when you feel like this is the last straw, finally the moment you are giving up and letting go. That is when you get to hold on as tight as possible to your hope.

Now, there are situations when the hope is gone. I hate even writing that out, but it's there. When someone refuses to work with you, to get help, to work things out for both of you. This is a two-way street – in a marriage – more in a more complex family structure, and if all sides are not willing to put in the work, it may be time to completely detach with love and walk away for your own sake and sanity.

I will say, for about the first year, my husband was not working to get help. He was going to meetings, but it was honestly to keep me happy – and he will tell you that to this day, no putting words in here. He went to meetings, and he was showing up there drunk. He was coming home from them drunk. He was drinking during the day. Hiding it still from me, because he was putting on this front that he was getting better and getting help. For the first year of our dating and married life, he refused to admit he had a problem and needed help. He kept telling me he would get it under control and left it at that. Then it was a birthday, or a holiday or some sort of other event and he would tell me after that he would get it together.

He really refused to do anything other than go to meetings for a very long time. And I thought I was crazy for keeping up the hope. We fought constantly and I was always on edge, anxious and had completely lost the trust. Especially once I found out he had been hiding it so he could drink more and not be responsible for it. We fought and yelled and all the things we were both trying so hard not to do. Still I kept up the hope. I have no idea how, and I really wish I could explain exactly how I was able to do it, but we all have ways to keep it up, we all have ways to stay in a certain mindset or to snap out of one.

I think the main reason I was able to keep up the hope is because I saw the person my husband was when he was sober. I truly felt like I knew and still know his soul, and he is the best human I have ever met. He is hilarious, and kind and truly wants to help people. His soul is the reason I was able to keep up the hope during the hard times. And I feel so lucky I was able to know him this way, and even more lucky I am able to continue to know him this way. Seeing more of that as he continues with sobriety allows me to keep up the hope, even in the bad times now. Yes, we still have them. If you have the opportunity to truly know your family member and to take a look at who they truly are, please do it. This could be the exact reason you keep up the hope in the toughness of addiction.

Then he went to detox. My hope levels soared. I was elated and so angry all at the same time, what a hard thing to attempt to describe. He finally was going to get real help and I couldn't let go of the anger. But I did keep up that hope. I felt so silly holding hope for someone that continued to relapse, or make promises, but there I was. I promise if you are keeping the hope, you do not need to feel crazy about it. Hope is such a beautiful thing to have. It keeps you going on those days you don't feel like you can go one step further. It keeps your mindset in a good place. Hope is beautiful, and it is okay to keep it up.

I kept up the hope and I am so grateful I did. Had I not, we would not be where we are now, which is a truly gorgeous place together. I know this is not the case in all situations, but I have so much gratitude it is the case in ours. So, yes, I am allowed to say I am grateful for all the shit of the past. I am so grateful.

Regardless of whether you are now where we are, you are still going through the pain and frustration, or you chose to make the decision to walk away, you can still have gratitude for what you have been through. I know it is tough to feel that way in the moment, but all the things you are going through, alone or together, are developing you into the person who can make it through. It is teaching you so many lessons and allowing you to help others who may need it. You can choose gratitude and make something terrible into something so beautiful regardless of the outcome. The choice is yours.

Chapter 22

Save the tracking for the post office

In the later years of my husband's active addiction, I would go to the parties, but on the happy face and laugh. Meanwhile I was counting each and every one of his drinks. I would watch as he poured, counting the seconds of how much liquor went in that glass. I would let him know I was ready to go and he would say, right after this drink. Sure. Not long later, he was attempting to sneak another one, but I had the watchful eye, no way was he sneaking anything. I would let him know again I was ready to leave, and again, after that drink. When we got home, I would always have something to say about the fact that he was pouring yet another before we went to bed – at 1am no less.

I was exhausted – from being up so late, from not getting enough sleep but mostly from tracking him all fucking night long. It was exhausting. And what was I really going to do about it? Yell at him in the middle of a party? No way. Shame him in to feeling guilty about it? I would certainly try to, but it wouldn't work on him, and it would make me feel worse and probably cause an altercation between the two of us that would result in yelling and hurt words.

I was a tracking machine. I would note what behaviors came up after 2, or 3 or 4 or 9. I would make a permanent mental note in my head so in the future I could figure out how many he had without even actually knowing the real count. And each drink showed a new behavior of sorts, a new mannerism, a new attitude. I am a bit embarrassed to admit it, but I learned to know this person better than I even knew myself at the time. I knew every move, every action, the way he would speak – just out of the right side of his mouth – the way he would laugh and how his eyes did these movements as if they were trying to focus. The way he would talk to himself, every single thing the drunk version of my husband did I noticed, and I knew.

I am a little embarrassed to say it because instead of working on myself and making myself better and learning to love me, I was so intensely focused on him and alcohol. The relationship he had with alcohol, I was intensely focused on how I could fix the problem, what I could do to control it, I was consumed with figuring out how to control the amount he drank. A task I would never accomplish because I cannot control it, or him. When I realized that is when I found freedom.

I would track every move he made, I would check receipts if I could find them, and trust me, if I had access to his bank account, I would probably be checking on that daily as well, more like hourly. Thankfully I did not have access, I would have driven myself crazier than I already was. I was making myself crazy, and allowing every bit of my brain to be focused there.

After a lot of time, intense therapy, so much practice in putting action to my words and thoughts, I learned that tracking is for the damn post office, not a behavior in your life. Tracking someone else's behavior is going to do nothing but bring you disappointment, sadness, exhaustion, anger, you name the negative emotion and it will probably come to your life during times of tracking. No matter how much effort you put forth you will never be able to control anything someone else does – catching on to that pattern – so the more tracking you do of someone else, the crazier it will make you feel.

I even got to the point of wanting to follow him places. Would he be at the gas station, what if I timed my commute to leave just two minutes after him and sat outside the gas station to see what he did. Would I find him buying alcohol? What if I left work just in time to watch him leave his office, would he head to the liquor store? Maybe the grocery store? Would I find him pouring alcohol in to a less suspicious bottle? He used to pour alcohol in to Gatorade bottles, or Dr. Pepper bottles so that no one would see them or know, but I did. I will not say these thoughts consumed me totally, it wasn't all I thought about, but it certainly was on my mind from time to time. And each time I had one of these thoughts, I knew how crazy they sounded. I knew I could never say it out loud because of that, because what the hell would people think if I admitted I felt the need to stalk my husband to find out if he was drinking. Just writing it seems crazy. But that is just it, this is crazy making. So many emotions come in to play and so many thoughts come in to play and it is all crazy making, except none of us are crazy. Not even close.

All that said, I never followed him anywhere. If he took off, I might drive past the bars near us to see if he stopped in, or to see if he was safe – so I told myself- but he was never there. That was the extent of my stalking skills. I never actually followed him around, but damn it took some willpower because I desperately wanted to. The part I couldn't understand was what if I did follow him and what if he did buy alcohol. What was I actually going to do about it? In the early days I probably would've screamed and yelled and do the whole ah hah! I caught you, son of a bitch!! It wouldn't help anything, it would actually make the situation worse, I know it would. And I probably would only threaten to leave, not actually do it, so what was I really hoping to accomplish here other than being correct? Other than throwing it in his face that I was right? Nothing. That was really all I was trying to accomplish, and what is that worth? In the moment, everything. Now, after so many experiences, so much knowledge and lessons gained, it is not worth it at all. My brain needs clarity, not to be mucked up with thoughts of what he is doing.

After all this time, I can finally understand I need to focus on me, and do what is best for me, not constantly worry about him and what he is doing. I cannot control what he does whether I know about it or not, so what is the point in all this tracking. What was the point in driving myself crazy counting and observing him to a fault to figure out how many drinks he had? I never enjoyed myself at parties we went to, I never enjoyed meeting new people or finding fun in the moments, or even finding joy. I never bothered myself with myself. I never bothered to stop and check if I was having a good time, I wasn't. I was never focused on me, or growing my relationships, or anything concerned with myself. I was entirely consumed with being bothered with him and everything he was doing. How healthy could that possibly be for either of us? Not at all.

How can you possibly be any good for yourself or to anyone else if you are not taking care of yourself? I am sure it is not impossible, but it would be damn hard, it was for me anyway.

Here is the real lesson here. I was no good. I was no good to me, definitely no good to him, no good to anyone else in my life. I put on the show, and the niceness and the smile, but I was no good to anyone. Behind all of it was this person longing for truth and trying everything she could to uncover it herself instead of letting it come naturally, being a nurturing person and being kind. Instead I was full of rage and anger, I was not very nice and being all kinds of fake. I was so unhappy it was insane. And the kicker was, that was on me. I was making the decisions that put myself in an unhappy place, I was allowing dishonesty to be so much a part of my life that it consumed me. All of this was on me.

I am not going to sit here and say that my husband's addiction was on me, I would never, that is his to handle. But, the unhappiness, the dishonesty, the loneliness and the solitude. Those parts were all mine. I was not detaching, I was codependent. I was not allowing myself to do things I loved, I was torturing myself trying to figure him out. I wasn't allowing myself space to heal and love, I was consuming that space with whatever he was going through. It was not fair to me. I was not being fair to me.

Again, I want to be very clear on this point, at no time do I, or want anyone else to take responsibility for things or actions that are not theirs. Never. But I highly recommend evaluating your own life, the way you feel, how you act and what you do and take responsibility for the parts that are unhappy, that make you feel like shit, that make you feel less. Take responsibility for it and do something about it.

I started focusing on me, I started doing things that made me happy regardless of whether he was there or not, I started bringing joy back in to my life and taking time for myself to heal and love my own being all by myself. You know what happened? I was happier, I was calmer, more settled and more confident in who I am as a human. I learned that I get to make the decisions in my life and if it isn't bringing me joy, I get to reevaluate what I am doing. I don't get to allow someone else to dictate how I feel or what I do. I don't get to allow someone else to determine how I live my life, and I don't get to lay the responsibility of making me happy on anyone other than myself. I also get to allow others to deal with their own actions in the ways they need to.

When we don't allow others to take responsibility for themselves, we are not allowing them to own their own lives, we are not allowing them to make mistakes and learn for themselves how to make it better, how to get better. It is unfair really. We get to learn how to detach to not only save our own sanity and lives, but to also save theirs. They get to figure it out on their own and so do you, and if that ends up leading you together, wonderful. If it ends up leading you apart that can also be wonderful. It all depends on your mindset.

Because here is another thing, I am never going to judge someone else's relationship, or their being for that matter. All of our experiences in this are different and for some people it will bring them closer together, and for others, farther apart. Whatever is better for the individual and couple in their own unique situation is what is best, and that is the end of it. I will always be supporting other women through this no matter what path they have taken in their relationship.

If abuse is happening, that is the only time I will heavily encourage someone to leave a relationship, other than that, I feel like we each can make our own decisions and once we find happiness and love for ourselves, we can reach it in the truest form, having that spill over in to all other relationships.

Chapter 23

Oh, contradictions.

Tainted love. Baby grand. Jumbo Shrimp. You know the ones, all the contradictions. That's what's up here.

Once I understood that I needed to focus inward and work on myself, I was somehow also able to comprehend that it would take some time to get up and running here. I gave myself grace and allowed for the times I would slip up and revert back to old, shitty behaviors. I learned slowly to forgive myself for fucking up in the past. I followed my own steps – from The Expedition book – and allowed myself the space I needed for growth.

I trudged forward and even when I would yell and scream and react instead of carefully responding, I felt awful afterward, but still allowed myself to just feel that and move forward. It was not easy, but I gave myself space and allowed myself forgiveness and grace.

Even with all of this, I still cannot figure out how I allowed all of this for myself, and coach others to do the same, but somehow expected my husband to just figure it all out in a day. I was not giving him any space or understanding any type of old, shitty behaviors to come back for him. If that happened it was a tragedy, it caused explosions and hurt feelings.

It was such a contradiction. I was doing all of this growth and learning for myself, but I wasn't allowing that safe space for my husband. If he fucked up, it was the end of the world. If he fell away from his program, I got paranoid and started questioning everything. I never gave him space for growth and I still hadn't figured out how to completely detach. Again, with the pressure.

I can't imagine how this must have made him feel, especially since I was the one going on about all the things I was learning and what I was working on to make myself better, and learning that fucking up was ok...for me. But not for him. Man, that must have made him feel like a pile of shit, wrapped in flies and placed on a mountain of shame. And he only let me know a little bit of that.

He was good at that, protecting me from what he was feeling as if laying it on me was some sort of burden. It wasn't. I wanted him to tell me all of the things, all of the feelings, I wanted him to lay it out right there for me. But how was he expected to when he would tell me the smallest detail of how he was feeling and then I would go on about how he should fix it, what he should do, and most of all what he was doing wrong. I pointed out what he was doing wrong over and over. As a note – he never pointed out what I do wrong, only when in a fight and he had nothing left to throw at me. He still doesn't point out when I am wrong, he just allows me to figure it out for myself, something huge I have learned from him. I get to let him figure it out for himself. When you constantly point out what someone else does wrong, how do you think that makes them feel? How would that make you feel? It would make you feel like shit, like there is nothing you could possibly do right. I have been there before, and I shocked myself every time I did it to him. Here's the thing, I did not think it was a bad thing, I honestly thought I was helping. Oh, the naivety.

So, on this mission to make myself better, I was also making him worse. Don't get me wrong, I wasn't going to stop working on myself, that is not the message here, far from it actually. But I was going to work harder on not pointing out when he wasn't doing something I thought was right. I was going to work harder on not pointing out his flaws, and not pointing out when he fucked up. He knew when he fucked up, he knew drinking was going to lead to our marriage falling apart, hell, he knew it would lead to his whole life falling apart, he knew all of that. It was up to him to figure out how to get better. It was all on him alone to figure it out. I could be there when he did, and support and encourage him, but in the end, this was all on him and had nothing to do with me.

Learning those words – it had nothing to do with me – was life changing. And confusing at the same time. But learning this made it easier to lovingly detach, and move forward in ways I needed to. It allowed me to practice some compassion and truly try to understand what it must be like on his end of things. Frustrating at times it didn't seem like he had the same thoughts on my end, but that is another issue we can get in to.

Seeking out compassion and understanding was the key to me realizing how much I was giving myself and how little I was giving him. While working on yourself is a seemingly full-time job, it doesn't mean you let your relationships slip, and it doesn't mean you stop caring about anyone but yourself. It also means practicing compassion and understanding for those around you. I was not giving him any space, nothing, for any mistakes he might possibly make. And there were several, and every one of them I made sure to make him feel terrible about it. Not to say there needs to be no accountability here and he can just do anything he wants without consequences, that is not what I am saying. There has to be a line drawn and just how much you will take, and what will happen if that line is crossed. What I am talking about here is the fact that we allow ourselves a certain amount of space for reverting back to old behaviors or screwing up, but we do not allow that same space for others in our lives. For me, most certainly for my husband.

It is so easy to say what you would do to fix something you are not going through because you are on the outside and you have the privilege of not being fully immersed in the issue, especially that of an addiction. I can tell you all the ways I would make it right, how I would seek help, what I would do. But I am not in the thick of addiction, so there is no way to tell whether I would actually do that or not. There is no way to understand fully what an addict is going through if you are not one. So, it is easy to say what I would do, and to beat him up over his fuck ups, and tell him all the ways he was doing something wrong, because I don't fully understand.

Why give ourselves slack and then not allow it for anyone else. We get to practice compassion for others and try to understand that everyone fucks up from time to time and how much we can handle of that and go from there. It is going to happen; I am almost positive at some point in your life you will fuck up. So why not allow someone some space for the same?

Chapter 24

Old Habits

Die hard. And I don't mean his, I mean mine.

I am going to talk about what just happened, minutes ago. I'll take you on the stroll of my day to day where I am relearning behaviors and trying like hell to shut down old ones. This is the daily thoughts of someone recovering from a loved one recovering from addiction – catch all that? Good.

I called my husband not too long ago to go over some details – we are currently working on the same project with our companies. I told him a bit about my day, it has been a rough one today, folks. We both get off topic and discuss our frustrations with one another and listened to one another. So much growth has happened this past year. We tell one another to have a better day and get off the phone.

Now, for the behavior pattern I get to work on. Just a few minutes later, he sent me a text telling me to put on my smile, and have a better day. Along with that text was a link to a very sweet song. Instead of feeling loved and appreciated and heard, I immediately went to the questioning aspect of my personality. In the past, the only time he sent me a sweet song link, was when he had been drinking. It was a tell tale sign he drank that day. It put me immediately on edge.

Now, I have had a ton of therapy, a lot of internal work on myself, marriage counselling together, so much work has been done. So, I knew I had the choice to appreciate the incredibly sweet gesture or dwell on it all day wondering if he had been drinking, ruin my entire day and wait until I got home to observe him as closely as I could for any other sign he had a drink that day. I know I have a choice in this. I know I get to figure out for myself how the rest of my day goes. I know I get to have hope and practice positivity, I know all of this at this point.

And it is so fucking hard. It is terribly hard to break the habit of the anger, the worry, the watchfulness. It is certainly not impossible, but damn it is tough.

So, here is the portion of my day. I decided to stay positive, to push through my day, focus on the tasks that I need to accomplish rather than what he is doing. I get to get things done for myself, my job, this book. I get to write and finish what I said I was going to finish, and what he did gets to go to the back of my mind, or out of my mind. And this time, I was successful. I went through the busy day, got done what was due and made my day the best I could.

Now, it is the following day. I am sitting at my computer reflecting on all of this and realizing I actually did it. I put it out of my mind, tough as it was, and got myself through the day. The shitty part is when I got home, I was all over looking for signs. I was watching his behaviors and his eyes, the way he talked. And guess what. Shut that shit down too. If he drank, he drank. There is nothing I can do about it at this point, other than control my own damn actions, not his. So, I did not ask him, though I really wanted to. I kept myself laughing and moved forward. Did he drink? Truth be told, I have no idea, but I really do not think he did. We had a great night and went to bed happy with one another. And I am super fucking proud of the day yesterday. Talk about some serious growth! Growth.....

Let's take this back to about a year ago. That's where my brain went when I realized just how much I had grown in everything that happened yesterday. I allowed myself some time to reflect on just how much growth had happened.

A year ago would have been a completely different story. Ill set it up for you: something nice happens and immediate questions set in. I would probably call him to hear his voice and confirm my suspicions. Then I would more than likely be an ass hole to anyone around me, including the people I work with – sorry old and current coworkers. Then I would drive home, and every single problem on the road would be his fault and fuel my anger. I almost couldn't wait to get home so that I could fight. And honestly the fight would be to prove I was right, because he would most likely lie about drinking. It would turn from anger at his addiction to anger at lies. And turn in to me wanting to prove he did and that he was lying. It was no longer about our relationship anymore; it was me versus him and me versus alcohol. It was me versus the entire world – or so it felt.

I would yell and fight and curse and not be a nice human in the least. I would turn our home in to a war zone, we both would at that point, but he was definitely the more passive one our marriage, which only infuriated me more. Eventually, he would start yelling back, just to be heard as well and hope to end the fight. It was so toxic and full of turmoil. The next day would end up being shitty because it was all I was thinking about, and there was a 99% chance we were not talking at this point. And probably even more of a chance he was still drinking, and I was still stewing about it.

What a way to live, right. Can you see the difference in a year ago and now? That is fully owed to me realizing I am also a problem, the way I approach our marriage is a problem, and I learned that I also need help and get to ask for help in my own recovery, with or without him continuing to drink. I learned I cannot control what he does – what anyone does for that matter. I learned I get to go to therapy and I get to find a community to help me. I learned our marriage is something we both get to work on, it was not failing simply because my husband was drinking. It was failing because neither of us were trying to work together.

Enter therapy and spouse recovery program. Enter self-love and taking care of me. Enter me taking responsibility for my own life. What a difference, when we focus on ourselves first and become better humans for ourselves. We end up becoming better in relationships and in the world in general.

I no longer allow someone else's action to take control of what I do with my day, or how I feel about my day. Do I screw up and think about those actions and have to pull myself back to the present? Yes. Do I still think about what I will say if I get home and realize he drank today? Yes. Does the worrying still hit me from time to time? Hell yes. This is work and it takes time. But I am getting better. So is he.

And I get to continue working and moving forward.

That is the beautiful part. He is doing the same types of things and I am relearning in that process that it was not something he did just because he had alcohol in his system, now he is doing it because he knows it will make me smile, and I will continue relearning my own triggers and behaviors surrounding the past. We cannot move forward until we realized what our problems are, not anyone else's. My issues and past thoughts around what he was doing is something I get to move on from and only I can do that, no one else can do it for me. Yes, he can continue to prove his sobriety and show me he loves me in these ways, and that definitely helps. But if I am not willing to move forward, I will stay stuck. And who the fuck wants to stay stuck? Not this girl.

What a beautiful thing, moving forward.

Chapter 25

Recovery goes both ways.

Just as someone with an addiction needs recovery assistance, so do the people in their lives – the spouses, family members, those closest to them – also need their own form of recovery.

I fought this for so long. In my head, this was his problem and he had to deal with it, it was not my problem. It was not my issue and I definitely did not need recovery. I was so wrong. And this is an instance I am happy I was wrong, and happy I was led in the correct direction by people who loved me and understood.

I started with Al-anon and honestly the first group I went to was a giant bitch fest of people just complaining about their spouses. It was the opposite of productive for my brain. It seemed so destructive and unhealthy. I went to two meetings and decided it was not for me. It actually was not until about a year later when I spoke about being married to an alcoholic, and a friend of mine approached me, that I finally decided to give another group a shot. And this was my group – I felt so accepted and it was such a loving and positive atmosphere, it was exactly what I needed. I even made time during the day to go, I used it as my lunch break from work since that was the only time this particular group met up. I implore you, it is so important, if you have a group you go to and it is not serving you to find one that does. And go when you can, but also don't sacrifice what the group can offer you for something else. It might be a little inconvenient on timing, but it will be worth it over and over for your well-being. Find one that makes you happy, serves what you need and is a positive space.

I also found an incredible spouse recovery program online. It was interactive through email and at your own pace to teach you about detachment, hope, and all things recovery. It helped me think about what was important to me and where I needed to focus more to feel better for myself and to understand that no matter what I was going to be okay. This program was with the Fearless Kind and I am forever grateful I was able to jump in with them. It turned my whole mindset around to a much better place and let me work on my own issues and my own triggers at my own pace without judgement. Also, it is run by two marriage and family therapists and so I felt like I was always in great hands and getting professional support. Plus, the emailing was so convenient for me, instead of a meeting or something that took time away from home or work, I was able to participate and learn as I went.

Therapy. So much therapy. Both individual and marriage therapy for the both of us to do together. This was imperative for our marriage. My husband also goes to individual therapy and now loves it. I am such a huge advocate for therapy because I know how well it really works. If you put your all in to it, with a completely open mind, listen and apply what you learn – apply what you learn is the most important part and the only way therapy is actually going to work – I promise you it will completely change you. There were times I was pissed off at my therapist, as was my husband, especially when we would talk about how we both work too much, because we both love what we do. But he was correct, we were allowing work to become the focus instead of our marriage.

Therapy was such a game changer since the day I started – and I actually started long before I even met my husband. It allows you to be in a safe, nonjudgmental space to share whatever you need to. Sometimes your therapist will just listen and other times they will give you some homework or some reflection questions to figure out why you are behaving or responding the way you are and discuss healthy ways to interact with others and with yourself. I credit the majority of my growth over the last 7 years or so to therapy.

Learning meditation and mindfulness. Holy. This takes a long time to get used to and practice, and it seems like sometimes I will never get it right. I still have to remind myself to make time for meditation and remind myself to be mindful, especially during times of stress. But learning how to manage both of these has been so detrimental to my own well-being and my recovery. Both keep me in the moment and present and stop me from spiraling down the hole from thoughts of the past or future, or better yet, things I cannot control. They both take a ton of practice and more often than not I take time to remind myself to practice mindfulness and schedule time to just be mindful, like on a walk and appreciating the things around me. They are not easy, but dang, when you put them to practice, they really change you.

Everything I have taken on as recovery I should have started long before I needed it. Everyone should get some therapy, and practice meditation and mindfulness, because at the end of the day, they just make you a better human all around. This isn't focused just on recovery, but on becoming a better human for yourself and for those around you. Honestly, I imagine a world where people are practicing all of this and it looks so beautiful! People are kinder to one another and more patient and definitely more understanding and compassionate. What a world.

Get you some help! Reach out, there is no shame and it will make you such a better person in the end, regardless of what happens in your relationship.

Chapter 26

Communicate.

Addiction thrives in a dull environment. It thrives on loneliness and darkness. It thrives when communicate is not present, and silence and depression take over. It thrives when there is not community.

So, we get to create the type of environment that addiction hates. One with community, and light and speaking our truth and communication.

I am amazed at how well my husband and I are able to communicate now. This was definitely not the case in the past. He did not know how to communicate really anything – his family does not really communicate their honest feelings with one another. And I didn't know how to communicate my anger – I only knew yelling, no other way to express anger or hurt or frustration or honestly happiness. Yes, I would yell my happiness as well. We were a mess. He became a deer in the headlights the second I mentioned having a conversation, and I would get frustrated by this and start yelling to get my point across. Que even more of the deer in the headlights look.

Just thinking about it now makes me so frustrated. If we had only known how easy communication is when we are calm and collected, we would have saved a ton of frustration and fighting.

We went to therapy and learned how to communicate with one another the way we hear one another. He hears me when I am calm and speak to him without adding the loudness to my voice. I learned I get to patient when I am speaking to him and make sure he is not distracted at the moment. Same with me, if I am distracted, he will get frustrated I am not listening instead of waiting a moment for me to finish what I am doing so I can give him my full attention. We have learned these small things we can do to be fully present with one another and make sure the other is hearing us.

If there is a hard conversation that needs to happen, we have learned to sit down and talk it out. I have also learned that sometimes he is just interested in what I am talking about and that is okay. I would get so frustrated when he would not find interest in what I had to say, thinking that because I had it to say and he was married to me, he should be interactive and interested. Not the case. And it is not the case with me either. Sometimes he talks about things I have zero interest in and I get to listen, but I may not always give feedback or ask questions, it is just not my jam. And that is okay for me, and also okay for him as long as we take the time for one another.

We also get to communicate our feelings around alcohol with one another. If I am feeling uneasy about something, I get to be honest with him and we have a conversation about it. As time goes on these have been less and less. Same with him, if he has a feeling about it, he gets to be honest with me and we can talk it out.

He also has learned to be honest and communicate his drinking. We have created a safe space and if he has had a drink that day, he gets to communicate that and have a conversation.

Communication is key to any relationship but especially one that includes addiction. The guessing game is brutal and will only leave things worse than they actually are. And if you can get communication down, I am certain success in a relationship follows. And not just communication from one end, but from both. Openly and honestly.

Learning how to communicate properly is truly what has saved our marriage, and continues to do so. And we continue working on it.

Chapter 27

Break to build.

Here is the big one. The big chapter. The most honest one yet. I have talked about gratitude to something that completely destroyed me. I have talked about how I can be thankful for this situation that made me question my entire life and left me defeated and deflated every single day. I have so much gratitude in my heart for it.

It is because I literally had to break to build. I had to be completely broken to get myself where I am today. A stronger, more compassionate, kinder and understanding person. I am much more patient, even when it seems like I am not. I have the capacity to love fully and to be compassionate that others are not perfect, and that others should not be expected to do what I would do. I am able to open my arms to those I wouldn't before. I have dropped judgement for the most part, I believe we will always be judgmental as humans, at least a little bit. I have developed a yearning to help others in a way I never experienced before, to be the voice of stability for them. I have a drive to show up to live authentically in the hopes that I inspire one other person.

I am a better wife. I understand more and respond instead of react to my husband. We have conversations instead of fights. We talk with one another, and we respect the hell out of each other for everything we have been through. We have a bond that is not easily broken because of everything we have been through and the foundation we have built. The trust is booming these days and we lean on each other for support instead of leaning away from one another.

So yes, all of the shit show, the bad nights, the embarrassment, the not wanting to tell anyone, the fights. All of it, is exactly what got me to where I am today and to be the person I am today, who is significantly better and working every day to be even better.

I owe it all to that shit show my husband and I lived through. I owe it all to my husband deciding to get help and being the person he knew he was all along.

I am grateful to have endured the shit show, and I am sure there is more to come in the future, we are not perfect. And this life is not perfect, even if it has nothing to do with alcohol. We will still have our issues and we are so much better equipped to handle them now, both with one another and just in life in general. This has built both of us up to be the people we need to be. So, when I say you are allowed to be grateful, I mean in the way I have allowed something terrible to become something beautiful. I have allowed a negative and frustrating narrative turn in to a beautiful message of hope and promise. I have grown immensely in the way I handle all things life – and I owe that to what I have learned in recovery, what recovery has taught me about myself and the person I want to be.

I would have never gone to Al-anon, a support system I don't think I could go without now. I never would have gone through the Fearless Kind program, which really was a lesson in how to handle life in general. And though I may have still continued therapy it would not have been specific to what I needed to become a better human, and I am so damn grateful.

I think of the lotus flower often in this case, how it has to grow through the thick mud under the water and make its way to the top of the water to bloom, it is such a grueling process that ends in a magnificent bloom. That is exactly what this is, what most of life is. We get through the thick mud and find there is a beautiful bloom on the other side.

My lesson here is don't discredit what got you where you are now. Whether that was a situation with an addict you had to navigate through, or something else of significance in your life. Don't allow it to just be something negative that happened in your life, really think about what good has come out of everything bad you have gone through, and I am going to guess if you have the right attitude and mindset, almost always something good comes out of it. There is a bloom after the mud, I am certain of it. And the person I have become is my bloom.

I firmly believe I had to completely break who I was to build who I am and who I will be. I couldn't be the person I needed to be if I stayed the way I was. I had to break to build. I had to push through the mud to get to the flower. I was nowhere near equipped to handle half of what I have gone through as the person I once was. I firmly believe everything we go through set us up for what and where we need to be, no matter how much it might hurt in the moment. The next time you are going through a hard season in life, think about that lotus flower and what you may be setting up for. Think about how you might need the hurt you are currently enduring so that you are better equipped for what is coming in the future, so you can handle it better, maybe with more patience – that is my story – or with more grit, or maybe you are finally able to speak your truth in your authentic voice, or maybe you will finally be able to walk away. Whatever it might be, every step of the way to get you there, you get to be grateful for.

Now, I am hesitant to be grateful to the late-night fights, the tears – sometimes crying myself to sleep or in to an anxiety attack – the screams, the terrible words, all of it. I am hesitant because those are moments, I am not proud of myself. And it may seem difficult to find gratitude for those moments, for me it is anyway, but I try to remember, I don't do those moments anymore. Or at the very least, they are few and far between these days because of how hard I have worked to make sure they don't happen. That is something to be grateful for, I no longer allow myself to have these types of reactions. That is something to be incredibly proud of as well.

The difficulty I think is to be grateful to anything dark in our lives. But the light will not come without the dark. All of it, we get to be grateful for. If you are no longer in a relationship with the addict in your life – be grateful you were strong enough to make a difficult decision. Be grateful for what you were taught in the process. Be grateful for every moment that lead you to the person you currently are. I can guarantee it is a better version of you than the past.

Think of the lotus. Thinking of breaking to build. You are becoming such an incredible version of yourself.

Chapter 28

Real time.

So here we are in real time. I am currently sitting at my kitchen counter – my favorite place to write, even though it makes my husband crazy – watching said husband make us kung pao shrimp for dinner and going over all the thoughts I have had the last few days.

I recently came home from a conference and you know what the best part about that was? I did not think about him drinking at all. I did not worry about him drinking at all. Now, he may still choose, even after all we have been through, to lie about it if he did. But, that's the kicker, if he does, he does. I know that no matter what, I am going to be okay. I have learned I cannot control his behaviors and actions, and stressing about doing that makes me nuts and not a fun person to be around. And I am a total fun person to be around, so why dampen that with something that is beyond my control? Not happening anymore.

If he did, I do trust these days he will be honest with me. Here's the thing with addicts, the truth always comes out eventually.

Always. If he drinks, well, that will come out eventually and, in the meantime, what am I going to do to myself? Stress and worry? No, sister, there is so much more in life to stress and worry about than someone else. I keep saying, marriage is hard, there is no need to make it harder. And that is my choice here.

This is what detachment is. I love him so much, and he gets to walk his own path as I walk mine, and we come together and it makes for some magic. We each get to live our own lives and not try to control the other, be honest with one another and help each other through the shit times.

Now, this is not saying all of a sudden our lives are sunshine and rainbows. Hell no. You know what we had to do? We had to learn how to fight and argue like normal adults in a relationship. Cause we all do it. We had gotten so used to blowing up at one another – more on my end than his – and we had to relearn how to actually argue like adults do. Like how weird is that? We had to learn that not everything gets to turn in to a huge blowout yelling fight, and sometimes you just have a disagreement and move on. We had to relearn how to communicate, and we are still learning more on how to communicate now and probably forever. Like what kind of couple has to learn how to fight the right way? Us, we did. And probably so many more couples involving an addict.

I had to learn to walk away – and make sure he understood that did not mean divorce – Lord knows I threatened that more times than I can even count. Divorce was my favorite word there for a while. Sorry, love. But that I just need a moment to walk away and get some clarity and finish our conversation, because surprise, surprise, I was getting too heated and had to take a step back. We had to relearn ourselves all over again.

I had to learn who my husband was sober. I got to relearn his quirks and the little things he does that reminds me of when he is drunk, and relearn how to adapt to who he is. And try like to hell not to be triggered when he acts a certain way. I got to relearn what his values and beliefs are and what he wants out of life. It has honestly been like learning a whole new human, one I knew was always in there and waiting to come out. But it was fucking scary, sometimes I just had no idea how to take him or how to talk to him. Or how to just not yell at him or treat him like shit. Who has to relearn that?! Me. I did.

And I get to relearn how to deal with my own triggers and stress surrounding his behaviors. There are definitely moments now when I question if he had a drink, this week in fact, I asked him. There was just something about the way he was acting. The way he was speaking to me and making jokes. And the way everything seemed to irritate him. So, I asked, he said no, and we moved on. I still have to keep training my brain to take his answer for what it is and not push any more. I still get to allow my brain to learn how to relax and stop overthinking every little move. I still get to train my brain to trust my husband and shut down the anxiety.

Oh, the anxiety. That one takes a while to go away, a long while, in case you were wondering if you were nuts. Nope. It just takes a long time to unlearn everything it took so long to learn. It takes a long time and a ton of work to move past all the anxieties, fears, mistrusts, behaviors, and start to relearn the addict in your life and how to love them properly. And it takes a long time for them to do the same. We get to give and receive grace in all areas with this. And that takes a lot of practice in itself, to give and receive grace.

I also got to learn what was enabling behavior and what was helpful behavior. The last thing I want to do is enable my husband, but sometimes our loving behavior is enabling them to continue. I also don't want to be a giant bitch when it comes to him either, so I get to learn balance in this area, and honestly, I think this will be work on my behalf until the day I die. I will constantly be working on improving myself, and my communication skills in all other relationships in my life. If we aren't growing, we are dying, right? I intend to grow as much as possible.

So, here we are in real time, over a year and half after my husband decided to get sober, and I am still working, so hard, to move forward from all the past. All the things we said to one another, the way we treated one another, the lies, the manipulation, the drinking, the relapses, all of it. It is a baby step by tiny little baby step process and as long as we keep moving forward together, it will only get better and better.

I can't talk about how long it takes to move on, because I have no idea. It's been well over a year, and I am still working on it. There are no promises I can make there, and no expectations either. Each day it gets easier and some days, it seems harder. But we work every single day. Both of us. We work together as a couple, and we work on ourselves as individuals. I am pretty solid in my thoughts that this is the only way this will work, if both people are on board, and both people are also working on themselves at the same time.

And, since it is common, sometimes marriages or relationships just don't stand up to this kind of pressure. And for those of you who have left your relationship, you are so damn brave.

You are so damn strong. You did what was best for you and in the end, it was leaving, and that takes a lot. I know you never asked for this, and you didn't want it, and now you have to deal with the aftermath – especially those of you with children – and that is also okay. I cannot say what my own future holds, and I hope you understand you have a place with me. Sometimes an ending is just better. For all parties. I am sending you so much love.

It also takes a tribe. This is not something you can go through alone, and reaching out is the first step. It is truly amazing the community that comes with this if you choose to put it out in to the world. So many people are dealing in silence and that is not okay. We all get to be here for one another and support and uplift one another to make it out on the other side. As people we tend to want to be so strong and hide any flaws (thanks social media) and make the world think everything is perfect. This existence is exhausting and not welcoming to those of us who need other people. I think we get to start welcoming others in to our world and talking about the issues we are having, we will feel less isolated and lonely, and actually problem solve together. How beautiful is that!

And I don't care what anyone says, unless someone has personally gone through what you are going through, they will never truly understand what it is like. People who have been in our shoes are who need, who we crave.

We also at the same time get to make the world a better place, a place of acceptance instead of mistreatment. A place of involvement and honesty and relationships and trust. What a powerful movement we could have if everyone just decided to tell the truth and help one another.

So, I am here. I will have your back and listen and be a friend should you need one.

And should I write a book in the future called Fuck it – my guide to getting out alive, well, you heard it here first and I am sure you will have my back through that as well.

Chapter 29

You are worthy.

There's nothing I'm not worthy of.

You are worthy. Of love, your emotions, your decisions. You are worthy of so much. And so am I.

Say it. Then say it again.

Firstly, you are worthy of love. You are worthy of beautiful love and all things fairytales are made of. That being said, life is not a freaking fairy tale and it might look a lot different than you imagined, but it is still beautiful. True love is always beautiful.

I think we get so caught up what love should look like and what we have been shown love looks like that sometimes we pass up real life love because it doesn't look the way we thought it would. I was always so caught up in what it would look like and what marriage would look like based on what I was told and shown, I thought my marriage and love was not good enough. I was always comparing what our marriage looked like to what other marriages looked like and wondering what was wrong. I was comparing the things he did with that of others and thinking it wasn't really love because it didn't look a certain way.

I also did not think I was worthy of a love that looked like the movies showed, or even some of my friends highlight reels. I thought maybe I had done something wrong or maybe I just did not deserve that type of love. With all the problems in our relationship, I hadn't realized that despite all of that, I really did have that type of love, it just looked differently than I thought it would, and at the time I did not think I deserved a beautiful great love, so I did not view my marriage in this way.

I thought that because my husband wouldn't give up alcohol for me, he did not love me enough, and therefore I was not worthy of love at all. It felt like if true love was there, he would give it up easily and appease me and want to make me happy. Since that was not the case, obviously the problem was me and how I did not deserve love. Oh, how false. And proof that this can really fuck up your mind. This is such a complex process and feeling worthy is part of that complex process on the side of loved ones.

So, once again, I went to work on myself. I realized the reason I felt like I wasn't worthy of love from someone else is because I did not love myself fully. Once I worked my own self-love, it became so clear I needed to love myself completely before I would feel worthy of love from someone else. I was not going to feel worthy of anything because I felt so worthless with myself on the inside.

Here is the secret: YOU ARE WORTHY. Right now, as you are, how you look, with the money you have, and the love in your heart. You are worthy just as you are, it is just up to you to believe that.

That's where I think most of make the biggest mistake in this whole worthy business. We expect to find it in the eyes of someone else. We expect someone else to tell us our worth, how lovable we are, what we can expect from them, all of it. We wait for someone else to tell us our worth. We wait for someone else to tell us if something is a good idea, or if an outfit looks good, or if we should do this or that.

If this book is stupid. Yep, I was waiting for someone ELSE to tell me whether or not this book was dumb, whether it would impact lives and maybe help someone. I was constantly waiting for approval on everything I did.

Que the fuckery in our marriage. His drinking told me I wasn't worth it. Ever. I wasn't worth getting sober for, our marriage wasn't worth working on, and I definitely wasn't worth the love he was giving me or not giving me. Total false bull shit.

Calling it out right now. I was worth it, because I said so. Me. All by my damn self. I was worth all the love in the world, my words were worth it. I just had to start believing that myself. I had to stop looking for what he was doing or what he thought to tell me my own worth. That is all inside me, babe. Much like his addiction having nothing to do with me, my worth had nothing to do with him, his behaviors or how he saw me at the moment. Because, let's be real, I was not always the nicest, kindest and most understanding person. Matter of fact, for a long time I was the exact opposite. I am okay with saying that because I made the choice to grow. I made the choice to see the worth in myself without him and his opinion. His drinking did not determine whether he loved me or not, whether he wanted to work on marriage or not, or whether I was worth it. His drinking was just that – his drinking. And it was a problem entirely of its own.

Once I made the choice to start seeing myself as worthy of all things good and prosperous was when my voice started to completely change. Regardless of what I was working on, how I looked at the time, what my opinions were, and a million other things that make me, me, I am worth it, and I am worthy.

I hate to break it to you, but feeling that worthiness, well, that's on you. No one else is in control of that and no one else can make you feel that way. Sure, they might make you feel good about yourself and that you are the reason the sun shines in the morning or whatever, but no one else can determine your worth in the world except you. Ill say it again for the cheap seats, no one in this world can determine your worth except you.

So get to work, sis. Start working on the things that make you worthy, the joys in your heart and what makes your brain happy. Start getting up and moving, start eating what makes your body feel good not just your taste buds, get rid of the dead weight and get on it. Your whole life is waiting for you and once you start to realize your worth in the world, there is nothing that will hold you back. Not even someone who didn't make you feel like you could.

The Bonus Chapter

The bonus chapter. The one I really wish I did not have the history, knowledge or experience to write. This is about the loss of someone to addiction. I wish no one knew this pain. But here we are and talking about it is important. Bringing light to the darkness is important. Creating a dialogue to break the stigmas, the negativity, the pain is important. And it is my mission to do just this.

I have been beyond broken by the effects of addiction, but no more so than the day I watched while one of the best friends in my life lost hers to addiction. I have taken my time to talk about this publicly and it is my hope that doing so will not only help me heal, but also allow others to know they are not alone and help them heal as well.

Alcohol is fucking bull shit. I went through a time where I wanted nothing to do with it, nothing to do with the people using it and nothing to do with hearing about it, drinking it, smelling it, or being near it. I isolated myself completely to avoid it. This was after her passing. The most bubbly, vibrant, frustrating, irritating, positive individual in my life.

I have moved past the hate for alcohol, I still have feelings about it, but I was angry and that anger came out at alcohol. And I allowed it to flow as much as it wanted to move past it. I no longer hate the substance, but I do hate the lack of knowledge around its dangers, the availability of it anywhere you go, the normalcy of drinking and the lack of education around the effects it has on humans. Her death allowed me to have my voice and speak it without fear of judgement and without really caring who thought I was on a high horse of some kind.

Here's the deal, I don't judge you. If you want to drink, by all means, live your life and do what makes you happy. If you cannot put it down, please get help. The deadly effects hit you quickly and there is no going back. If you need help and are scared to reach out, please reach out to me, this is a safe zone and I am here for you.

So, let's dig in. If this pisses you off at all, if you are offended or think I am on some sort of high horse because I have chosen to stop drinking, please take a look in the mirror and ask yourself why you feel that way. It is not because of me. Like I said, I do not judge you or your life. I want to make that as clear as I possibly can.

Alcohol, regardless of how normal we have made it, is a drug. Specifically, it is a depressant. We are so quick to jump to medications for depression but my first thought would be to decrease the amount of depressants you are taking in on your own if your life first. But I digress. I could talk about this all day.

It is a drug, and those of us who are able to have a drink and put it down are privileged to say the least. Those who can watch commercials on television promoting alcohol, day drinking, and how fun it is and not know the other side of it are lucky to not know the effects it has. That is why more conversations are needed. We only see the good and fun side of alcohol. We do not see the devastating effects it has on some. We do not see the people in the emergency room begging someone to save their lives only to go through the dangerous process of detox just to start all over again because it takes over their brains. We don't advertise the person crying and contemplating suicide because they have lost everything and everyone in their lives and they cannot understand why they have allowed a substance to get them to this place. We do not see the reality of someone losing their life because they did not seek help in time to get well. We do not make commercials about people feeling worthless because of addiction or feeling so shamed by it they hide. We do not talk about societies lack of compassion when it comes to addiction and ignoring it. We do not talk about these things because we don't want to see the ugly side of something we enjoy in mass and have fun with. We do not want to see that side because it is easier not to. It is easier to assume this only happens to bad people. It is easier to assume people can just stop and control themselves and that addiction is their fault and their choice. It is easier to ignore so we can justify our behavior. It is easier to say, that would never be me. It is easy to judge.

But for those of us who have lived to see all of it, it is far from a joke. It is far from easy to ignore it. The damaging effects last a lifetime, the mental damage lasts forever. And in some cases, the physical damage does as well.

It has been seven months since I sat in a hospital room with other friends and family and waited for one of my best friends to die. It has been seven months since we watched her take her last breath, and cried together as her family asked us for privacy. It has been seven months and I am still angry, hurt, frustrated, angry, devastated. I can list every emotion. It has been seven months and I still see her show up for me in places I never would have guessed. It has been seven months and I still grab my phone to call or text when something happens and relive the pain of realizing she is not here with me any longer.

Long before this I had already become frustrated with her and drinking. I had been through so much involving alcohol and I was just done with it. I had stopped drinking and she was really proud and happy for me and talked about stopping herself. There is not a day that goes by now I wish I would have taken that more seriously and helped her more. I wish I would have pushed her to detox and go to meetings. I wish, I wish, I wish. But the truth is, no one is going to stop unless they want to, and in her case, I really don't think she wanted to yet. It was months before that she was in the hospital and then out and then back in. It was her birthday when I finally went to see and realized how bad it actually was and asked a million questions to try to understand what was happening. It was a night in my garage when my husband told me to prepare to lose her. He was crazy, there was no way that was happening. Sixteen days later, it did.

I wish this pain on no one on this earth. There is no understanding, there is no closure, and there is a ton of fucking judgement. When you attempt to plan a memorial so that there is no alcohol available for it. When you turn your head when someone makes a joke about their liver being a champion after drinking all weekend. When you try like hell not to cry when someone tells a story that involves her drinking. When you keep your cool instead of throwing something at the wall when someone talks about how much she drank. When you beat yourself up for not doing more and not stopping it, as if you could.

This is the ugly side of alcohol. The one no one wants to know and definitely no one wants to talk about, and everyone wants to judge. It is the side I will fight like hell for people to see, so they understand exactly how dangerous it truly is and to practice caution. The pain associated is not worth it.

I miss my friend. I miss her daily. I miss the way she would talk to me, the way she made people laugh, the way her giant smile would light up the room, the way she pissed me off almost daily, the way she thought she knew better about my life than me, the way she was my biggest cheerleader no matter what, the way she would call me, the way she was always there for me, the way she always tried to get me to see the other side of every situation, the way she pissed me off daily (that one deserves a second mention, because it was seriously daily).

Because of all the ugly I have seen, my choice in life is to not drink. And I want to encourage everyone to do a little more research, have a little more conversation, try some compassionate understanding when it comes to alcohol. The more light we bring to darkness, the better, the more conversation we bring to any issue, the more understanding there will be and the more people will feel comfortable enough to seek the help they need.

And, for the love of all that is holy in this world, please stop pushing people to drink when they say no. Please stop asking questions someone might not want to answer. If someone declines alcohol, please just say ok and offer them something else. If they decline an invitation to a bar or party, please try to understand that may not be something they can do right now.

And know this, someone you know is having an issue with alcohol, and they may not feel like the can talk to you about it. Be careful how you speak about alcohol and those who may have an issue with it, you may be closing the only door they have to get help. And please be open to having a conversation with someone and do not assume they are a prude or judging you, they may just need someone to talk to, and you might just be that person.

I wish you all so much love and light that darkness cannot get in.

Solid resources to have....

<u>A therapist.</u> Call your insurance or ask around, someone you know has one and will be happy to refer you. If you are in the Las Vegas area, send me over an email and I will send you my favorites.

<u>Al-Anon:</u> https://al-anon.org/

<u>Fearless Kind:</u> https://www.fearlesskind.com/

<u>Substance Abuse and Mental Health Services Administration:</u>

SAMHSA's National Helpline, 1-800-662-HELP (4357), (also known as the Treatment Referral Routing Service) or TTY: 1-800-487-4889 is a confidential, free, 24-hour-a-day, 365-day-a-year, information service, in English and Spanish, for individuals and family members facing mental and/or substance use disorders. This service provides referrals to local treatment facilities, support groups, and community-based organizations. Callers can also order free publications and other information.

<u>Books that helped me:</u>

Embracing Detachment by Karen Casey

Eight Dates by John Gottman, Phd and Julie Shwartz Gottman, PhD

AMBER HAEHNEL

My shameless plug: The Expedition by Amber Haehnel

Do You Expedition Companion Workbook by Amber Haehnel

Podcasts I recommend:

Recover Everything – recovereverything.com

Armchair Expert – armchairexpertpod.com

Freedom Obsessed – sarahcookcoaching.com/podcast

About the Author

Hi, I am Amber.

I am an anthropologist, and obviously a writer.

I am married to a fantastic dude who is in recovery, at the point of publication he has been sober for about 7 months, and started his recovery almost two years ago.

We live in Las Vegas with our three super cool dogs.

I realized through our marriage and his recovery I also needed my own and started my own journey on finding that recovery. I sought out therapy, meditation coaches, mindfulness practices, yoga, tarot, all the things I possibly could once I realized I had my own issues to get through.

With that was born the self-love twelve steps, The Expedition. After releasing that book, I had so much feedback and people reaching out I decided to share my journey through his recovery here in Breaking the Silence.

Writing creates a release and outlet for me nothing else does and allows me to spread awareness and have a voice in all of this, and give that voice to others who need it.

I hope this book has helped you in some way, whether you are in a relationship with someone like I am, or got some clarity on what it might be like.

Made in the USA
Las Vegas, NV
14 March 2023

69077024R00100